Kudensho: Secrets of Karate

Kazumi Tabata

Insights and Refinement in Karate
from the
Author of *Secret Tactics* and *Mind Power*

Library of Congress Control Number: 2010943468

ISBN 0-7414-6416-0 Paperback
ISBN 0-7414-6417-9 Hardcover

Printed in the United States of America

Published February 2011

INFINITY PUBLISHING
1094 New DeHaven Street, Suite 100
West Conshohocken, PA 19428-2713
Toll-free (877) BUY BOOK
Local Phone (610) 941-9999
Fax (610) 941-9959
Info@buybooksontheweb.com
www.buybooksontheweb.com

Kudensho: Secrets of Karate

Kazumi Tabata

Insights and Refinement in Karate
from the
Author of *Secret Tactics* and *Mind Power*

FOREWARD

Looking back at the history of Japanese martial arts, we see that the art was perfected by the warriors who wagered their lives on the battlefields during the era of the Warring States, and who reached the ultimate limit of bringing together heart, skill and body.

To have the body and weapon become one, and to have skill be in action simultaneously with the heart's workings, are the realization of the state of nothingness.

One can train his body to become as sharp as a weapon, and if so it will matter little should he lose his weapon in battle. When he combines spirit, body and technique into one, he attains completeness in martial arts.

As we will discuss within this book, the character for "kara" in Kara-te-do embodies the heart and wisdom of nature. An entire world exists that cannot be perceived by the body and its senses, but only through perception of the heart. When one comprehends the harmony of the universe, one can demonstrate miraculous strength and skill.

When God, nature, one's rivals and oneself all become one, the heart and skill reach maturity, and great strength is demonstrated without premeditation or thought. Without this, hesitation and uncertainty will diminish skill and strength.

Every person thinks that his/her own path (school, art form, religion, etc.) is the best, but wisdom has only one pinnacle. The paths to true wisdom and enlightenment are many, but it is important not to be held captive by the path itself.

This book reveals and explains for the first time the original meaning and training methods of karate-do. While it shows basic techniques and their applications, it is not simply a primer for karate. It is both a message and a journal from a predecessor to future generation. Karate can be considered the origin of all martial arts. If this book is of use to the reader, it will be my honor indeed.

Gasshou,

Kazumi Tabata

About the Title

The title, "Ku Den Sho," is comprised of three words. "Sho" simply means "book." "Ku" actually has several meanings that are applicable to the message of this book. As described within the first Chapter 1, Volume I of this book, "Ku" is also an alternative translation of the character for "Kara" in Karate. Finally, "Ku" in a completely different context refers to "secrets." "Den" refers "passing on" of truth as in father to son, generation to generation. Thus, "Ku Den Sho" is intended to mean "A book in which Secrets of Karate are revealed." Herein, we pass on both basic techniques as well as advanced aspects of Karate that have in the past typically been handed down in a more private setting.

Karate has evolved considerably since its inception, and must continue to do so to embrace our changing environment. Great advances in the art were made by Gichin Funakoshi, the founder of Shotokan Karate and considered by many to be responsible for spreading the art throughout the world. We include herein advances and refinements in Karate that have continued to the present day, and encourage you to continue the evolution of karate.

Recommendation

I have had the honor and benefit of training with Master Tabata since 1974, after seeing an amazing demonstration by him and his students at UMass•Boston.

Master Tabata maintains strong classical roots, yet brings new life to the Art. Training with Master Tabata provides a physical, mental and spiritual lift that can help one face and overcome adversity wherever and in whatever form it may arise.

I recommend "Kudenso: Secrets of Karate" as a guide for the novice practitioner and a reference for seniors. College Karate Clubs can use this book as their syllabus. I also recommend Master Tabata's other books, "Secret Tactics" and "Mind Power" (available from Tuttle Publishing), which expand upon the philosophical aspects of Karate that are introduced within Kudensho.

Thomas B. Shea, Ph.D.
Professor & Director, Center for Cellular Neurobiology
University of Massachusetts Lowell
President, North American Karate Federation

CONTENTS

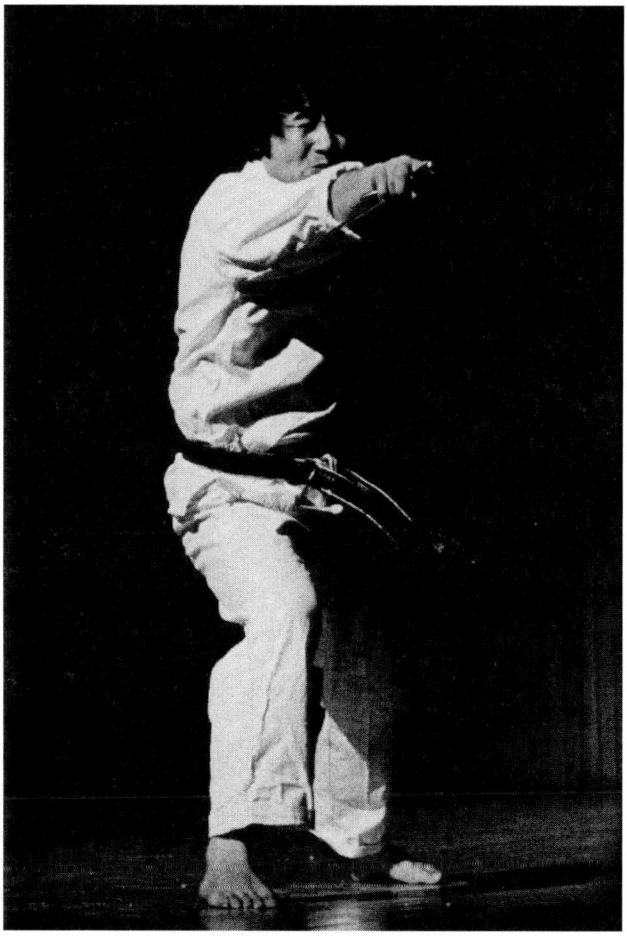

VOLUME I:
Basic Knowledge

Chapter 1:
Proper spirit for training

What is the Essence of Studying Karate?

Studying karate means learning and mastering high-level self-defense techniques that have been created from centuries of battle experience. It is said that those who thoroughly study and practice karate attain a kind of enlightenment, which transcends life and death. The skills displayed after attaining enlightenment become fulfilled with a spirit, which is one of balance between nature and the universe. This enlightenment is the same as that achieved in Zen Buddhism. Zen enlightenment is reached through quiet meditation; karate enlightenment is achieved through action. This is why karate is called "Moving Zen".

People who practice karate naturally become polite, wise, truthful, tough-minded and loyal; at the same time they achieve physical strength. Karate helps to overcome troubles and fear, and enables you to build a strong body and mind. It helps to cultivate healthy convictions and control ego so that one can get along with others. If somebody attacks, you should be able to fend off the attack gently, without a major confrontation. When there is no alternative to fighting, you should be able to defeat your opponent in one blow.

If karate is to help you in daily life, it is extremely important not to become arrogant or vain. Just as it is said "a healthy spirit dwells only in a healthy body", karate can be practiced only when proper etiquette is followed. You learn high-level techniques while building your character. Through the continual practice of basic techniques, the essence of karate can be realized—a complete unity between physical and spiritual understanding.

Manners and Attributes of Karate Practice and in the Dojo

What is a *Dojo*? Many of us have heard of the place where martial arts are taught, a dojo. In actuality, a dojo is place where one seeks truth, trains one's mind and perfects one's techniques. It is a sacred place to learn reason and a sense of obligation. The word dojo comes from the place where Shaka Buddha started Buddhism, and subsequently, derives its meaning for those who enter it. Anyplace, whether it be the in the midst of the mountains, near a beach, in a corner of a garden, field or inside a house, can be a dojo if one uses the place properly. For perfection in karate, as in any art, it is necessary to have several aims, proper attitudes, and to nurture one's mind in the place decided upon as the dojo.

Pay close attention to the following principles:

(1) Make an effort to keep the sacredness of the dojo and to practice sincerely.

(2) Leave behind confusion and the disturbances of everyday life to concentrate on practice.

(3) Maintain a sincere and humble mind and avoid arrogant behavior. Do not throw out careless words or look down upon others, or upon oneself. Be careful not to make others feel unpleasant.

(4) Try to accept other's opinions with a generous attitude.

Manners in a Dojo:

(1) Repeat each technique carefully and patiently, and make an effort to perfect your techniques.

(2) Deepen your theoretical understanding of techniques through careful study.

(3) Carry out your study rationally, to comprehend and to come up with your own ideas.

(4) Try to respect the theory and experience of predecessors.

(5) Learn from the strong points of others and make up for one's own weak points.

(6) Try to create peace among karate colleagues and trust in each other.

(7) Treat junior members with kindness, yet instruct them strictly.

CHAPTER 2
Proper Practice and Attitude

1. Proper practice and attitude for karate

Practice in karate is intended to develop stability, freedom, responsiveness, endurance and effective power; also to enable a student to use technique instinctively. Methods of practice are largely classified into the following groups:

a. Basic Exercise
b. Reciprocal Exercise
c. Supplemental Exercise
d. Trial Training

The four methods of exercise are explained in detail as follows:

a. Basic Exercise

(1) *Stationary Exercise* – This is a method for acquiring correct technique by oneself, or with another student. Without changing position, one emphasizes basic techniques, concentrating on accuracy and stability. "Stationary blocks and strikes" (sonobatsukiuke) are good examples of this type of exercise.

(2) *Mobile Exercise* (forward and backward) – A method in which one practices each basic technique while moving in a straight line back and forth. Both stability and freedom of technique are stressed.

(3) *Rotation Exercises* – Performed repeatedly while turning, such that one faces in each of four different directions. Both freedom and responsiveness of technique are emphasized. Good examples are the "Blocks and strikes in four directions" (shihotsukiuke).

b. Reciprocal Exercise

(1) *Pattern Exercises* - in which two students perform various techniques from a series of positions on the basis of set patterns. They practice offensive and defensive moves in each situation, and in doing so enable themselves to see technique effectively.

(2) *Free Exercises* in which students freely confront each other with various movements, standing at fixed positions and using a continuous series of offensive and defensive techniques.

(3) *Game Exercises* in which students pay the utmost attention to gaining points while using simple, continuous, and

complex techniques. It is designed for learning tactics for game maneuvers in each position.

(4) *Form Exercises* in which two students actually come to practice the series of motions that make up a particular form. One student takes the role of performer, the other of assistant.

c. Supplemental Exercise

(1) *Special Conditioning* – the main purpose of which is to raise the degree of skin toughness and bone resistance. This training uses various tools and instruments to strengthen particular parts of the body applied in certain movements.

(2) *Strength Training* – Places major importance on raising the muscle's absolute strength, sustenance, and contractile power necessary for a particular technique.

(3) *Speed Training* – By increasing a student's speed, his ability to recognize and anticipate an opponent's attack becomes a natural reflex. An awareness of movements as well as stance is a key requirement during all phases of speed training.

d. Trial Training

This method aims to test one's power and speed experimentally. Certain parts of the body are strengthened in order to gain effectiveness in particular techniques.

2. Exercise Methods Depending on Differences in Physical Strength and One's Purpose

Karate exercises can be characterized by posture and action as follows:

1. Low Stance
2. Middle Stance
3. High Stance

(1) *Low Stance* means that one's feet are spread at shoulder length, with the knees bent, and the arms and upper body stretching freely. This is an adequate position for basic training. It will help one to understand precisely the correct use of space and technique. This method is good for a young person. Someone who learns the martial arts can start with the Low Stance and build up a good basis.

(2) *High Stance* is a style that sets the feet narrowly and involves small fine acts. The main objective is practical application.

(3) *Middle Stance* is a posture between Low Stance and High Stance. It is advisable for a young person to start from Low Stance, but it is good for a person of middle age, or one who is in weak physical condition, to gradually move from Middle Stance to Low Stance. In this case, it is important for an older person never to try to go beyond his or her ability. However, it goes without saying that a lazy person cannot gain good health, and that one cannot cultivate strength, health, or good technique without effort.

3. Take Advantage of One's Own Physique

One must develop techniques in accordance with one's physical capacity and characteristics, and must be able to apply these techniques in one's own way. For example, a person who is small and quick should learn offensive moves in which he turns aside his body and performs from a lower level. One who is light with springing power should develop his jumping. Thirdly, a big heavy person should develop offensive moves making reverse use of his opponent's actions.

4. Eliminate Bad Habits

Be careful to correct bad habits – they can become a cause for disaster later on. Typical habits become associated with particular actions, and if they show up often in competition your opponent will learn to recognize them, putting you at a disadvantage. Be careful on this point.

5. Mental Preparation and Attitude before Practice and a Contest

The practice of correct karate must follow fundamental principles. It is important to start practicing with a relaxed mind, to acquire strength with the correct posture and to gradually increase strength so as to apply techniques freely. There are some people who believe that one performs karate vigorously and with all one's power, but this is not true. Putting all of one's power into performance is the sign of a beginner. Anyone who does not fully bear in mind the methods listed here will fall into error.

6. Mental Preparation

(a) Correct technique should become a habit. For this purpose one should faithfully practice each technique, advancing from one stage to another, and then move to the next point in the technique. This method of perfecting one technique at a time is more effective than trying to acquire many techniques at once out of curiosity and impatience.

(b) One should start advanced and applied techniques only after fully mastering the basic techniques. Over-ambitious actions will bring on poor results and within two or three years one's capacity to improve will be exhausted.

7. On Teacher and Student

Karate can be acquired not with money but with heart. Only if a teacher and student respect each other and make contact, without forgetting courtesy between each other, will their relationship be long-lasting. It is important in learning karate that the teacher teach the student sincerely, and the student sincerely learn from his teacher. The basics, especially, should be learned well and taught with care. Once the basics are achieved firmly, one can add as much as he or she wants. *A good teacher will withhold none of his knowledge from a good student.*

8. Some suggestions for Karate Clubs in Schools and Colleges

(a) Role of Karate and the Student

Because the school karate club member already looks upon himself as a student, he should value karate more for its discipline and training than as a fighting technique.

(b) Scholarship and Karate

Needless to say, studies should always take precedence over karate. But if you practice karate in your free time, you will acquire something that will serve you for your entire life. During your participation in the karate club, once or twice try to push yourself to the limits of your physical abilities. This will help you to know your limits and will help you in overcoming hardships later on in life.

(c) Harmony and Group Participation

A person joins a karate club in order to improve his skills, but he also learns how to participate in groups. This will help him later in life.

(d) Relations Between Junior and Senior Members

Members should be careful of interpersonal relations, harmony being of the utmost concern and importance. Unity and group strength are achieved when the group shares pleasant and sad moments. Various people should be appointed to handle club affairs, and leaders should see that the appointees dispatch their duties properly. If a problem should arise, the coach or club president should report it to the proper authorities and take remedial measures.

(e) The Coach

The Coach is appointed with the approval of the club president and the proper school authorities. He has charge of the technical aspects of the club's affairs and is also responsible for the improvement of the members' personalities. He is not responsible for the management of the club.

(f) Overall Responsibility

The club should see that it maintains and preserves proper karate forms and techniques. This is the responsibility of each member; it is wrong to rely solely on the senior members.

9. How to learn

In Karate-Do, first you learn technique. Next, you begin to apply correct breathing to your technique. As training continues, you will begin to gain physical strength. Finally, you will gain mental strength. However, it is important to try and combine your mental and body strength in your techniques, which will help you obtain a "heavenly power." The Japanese term that describes this power is "mu." When you operate at this level, you do not have to defeat your opponent; rather, you in a way let him defeat himself. Your technique comes out naturally, without thinking. Your opponent will seem to move slowly.

10. What are Martial Arts?

Budo, which literally means the "way of stopping conflict" implies the path towards learning two things: knowledge of technique and knowledge of soul. This knowledge should be both rational and practical, and should apply to any field. You need the ability to comprehend, react and move quickly, with good technique.

11. Proper Method for Putting On the Belt:

(a) Locate the center of the belt, and place it low across your abdomen (about three finger-widths below the navel).

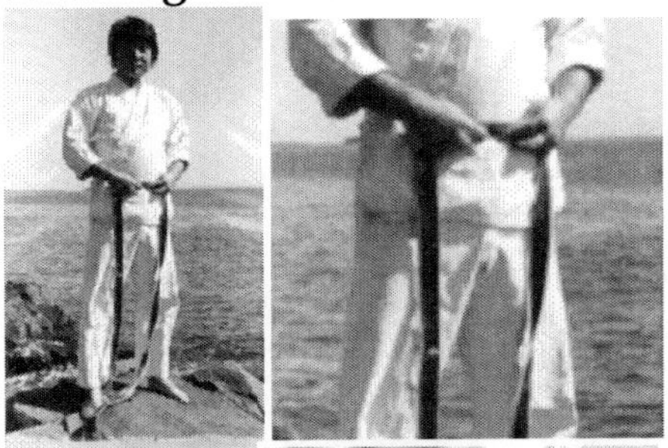

(b) Cross both ends of the belt behind you and bring them around in front, with the left side on the top.

(c) Bring the left "tail" underneath all of the belt wrappings and pull it over the top.

(d) Wrap the new left "tail" over the right tail and tuck it through the resulting loop, being careful not to twist either tail.

(e) Pull both tails in a downward manner to tighten the knot.
(f) If you have performed this correctly, both tails will hang in a downward manner.

11. Proper Method for Folding the Gi (Karate Uniform)

(a) Arrange both the top and bottom flat on the floor.

(b) Fold the pants along the leg and place along the center of the top.

(c) Fold each sleeve to the center.

(d) Fold each side of the top to the center.

(e) and (f) Fold or roll the gi along the line of the bottom.

(g) Wrap and tie the belt around the gi as you would if you were putting on the belt (see previous page). Note: Alternatively, the belt can be inserted before step (f) to avoid displaying rank.

12. Proper Way to Bow

The spirit of the bow is found in many situations. It is important for beginners to learn when to bow, and for all students to continue to bow and faithfully follow proper dojo etiquette.

a. Prepare before each practice by meditating and clearing your mind.

b. Upon entering the dojo you must first bow at the entrance and then to the instructor.

c. If the instructor arrives after the students, the senior student should call for attention and have all the students bow and greet the instructor.

d. As you leave the dojo you should bow to the instructor and bow to the dojo.

How to Bow from a Natural Stance

VOLUME II: Basic Techniques

CHAPTER 1
FUNDAMENTALS

The fundamentals of Karate are composed of those for attack (punches, strikes, and kicks) and those for defense. Mastery of Karate can be attained only through repeated practice of these fundamental techniques. Efforts should be made to attain proficiency in the fundamentals while always keeping in mind that your opponents are also making efforts to be faster, stronger, and more accurate than you.

1. HANDS

1. Stretch out four fingers together, with the thumb kept apart.

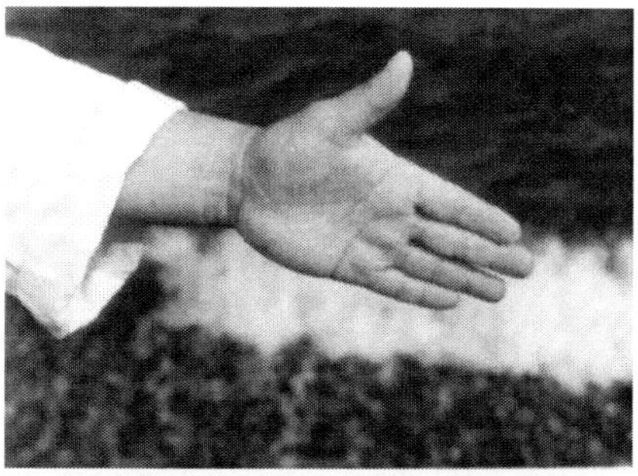

2. Lightly clench the little, ring, middle, and index fingers into your palm.
3. Roll down all the four fingers tightly into the palm of your hand.
4. Anchor the fingers by pressing your thumb tightly downward against the index and middle fingers.

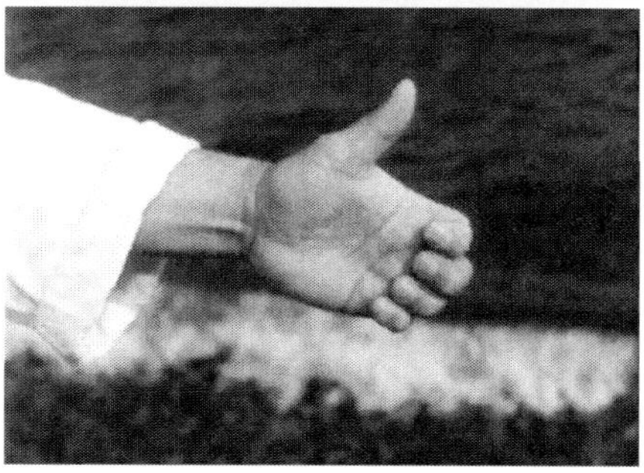

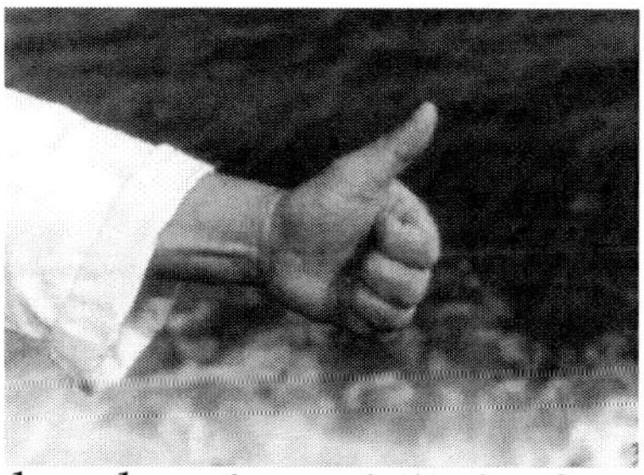

Try to tighten your fist with the thumb and little fingers pressed inward. In no event should the pressure of the little finger be released; otherwise (1) your fingers could be sprained, and (2) the potential power of your fist would be greatly reduced.

2. SEIKEN (FOREFIST):

1. The knuckles of both the index and middle fingers should hit the target at the same time.
Hold your wrist and forearm straight and be sure to keep your wrist from bending when you hit the target.

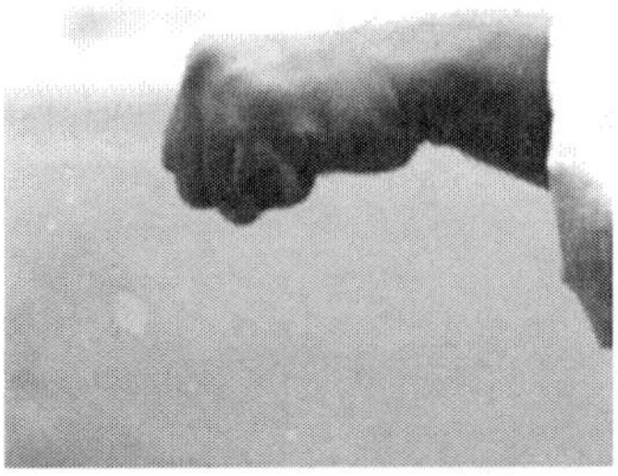

2. When viewed from the side, the index and middle fingers should be vertical.

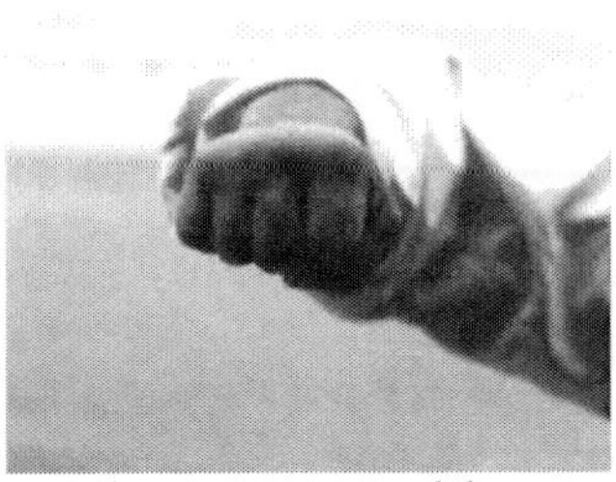

The Seiken is used extensively and can be improved by training with a punching board (see Chapter 9).

3. URAKEN (BACKFIST)
Use the back of the seiken (Forefist) to attack the face of your opponent.

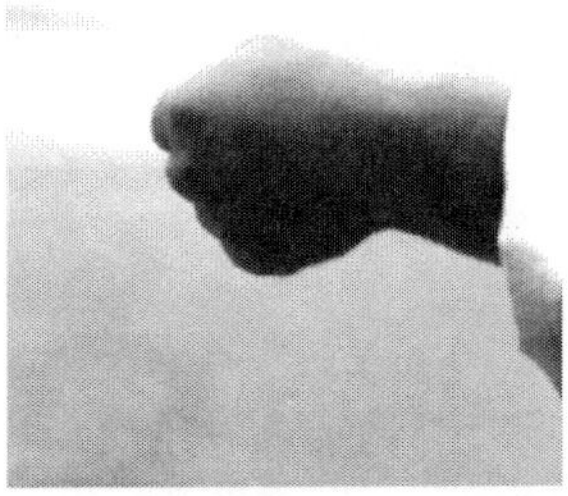

4. TETTSUI (IRON HAMMER OR BOTTOMFIST)
Use the bottom, namely the little finger's side of the fist to attack your opponent's face or limb joints, or to defend against attacks. The principle employed is the same as that for a hammer.

5. IPPON-KEN (FIST WITH PROMINENT KNUCKLE)

There are two ways of clenching this form of fist.

Nakadaka-Ipponken This is modified form of a forefist (seiken) with the knuckle of the middle finger raised. This is useful for attacking your opponent's face, upper lip, temple, brow, solar plexus and throat.

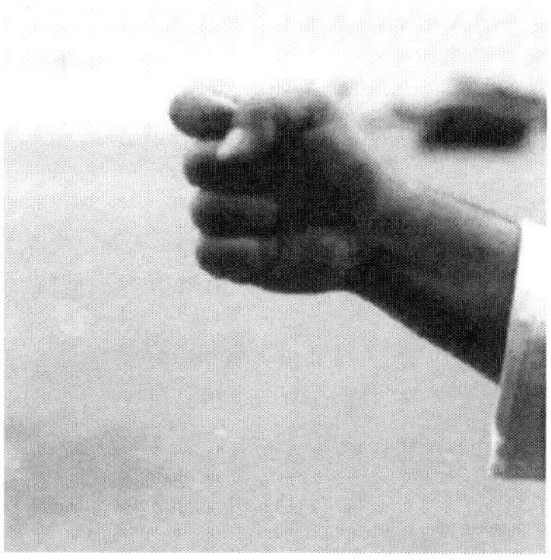

Ipponken Clench the fist with the knuckle of the index finger raised, while holding the raised finger firmly with the thumb. The use of this fist is the same as for the Nakadaka-ipponken in (1) above. *With the Nakadaka-ipponken and the Ipponken, clench the fist firmly by holding the raised the knuckles with the thumb. Don't release the pressure of the little finger.*

6. HIRAKEN (SHALLOW-FIST)

Clench your fingers shallowly, and use the prominent portion of the second joints of the four fingers to attack. Hold the thumb pressed firmly against the side of the index finger. Use to attack your opponent's temple and upper lip.

7. SHUTO (KNIFE-HAND)
Extend the four fingers and hold the thumb slightly bent. Use the outer edge of the hand to attack. Use to defend against attacks to your arms and legs, and to attack your opponent's temple, brow, and neck.

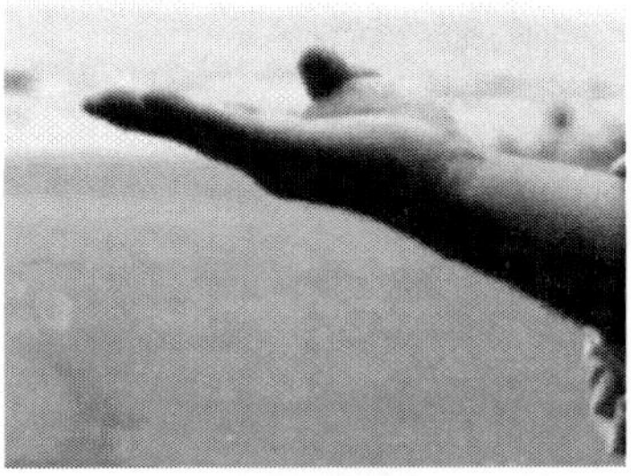

8. UCHIKEN (INNER FIST)
Use the inside of your wrist to attack your opponent's jaw.

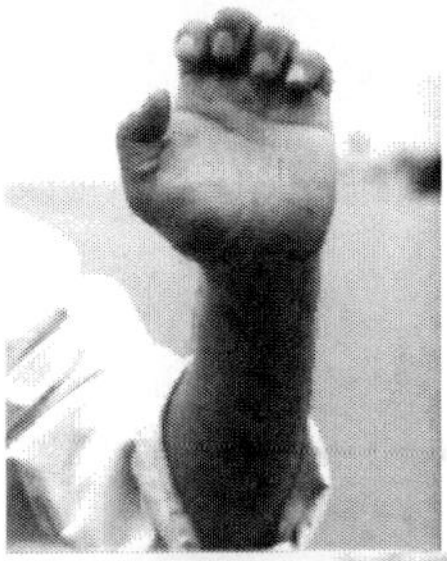

9. HAITO (REVERSE KNIFE HAND)
Use the other side of shuto (the outer edge and base of the index finger) to attack your opponent's temple and neck.

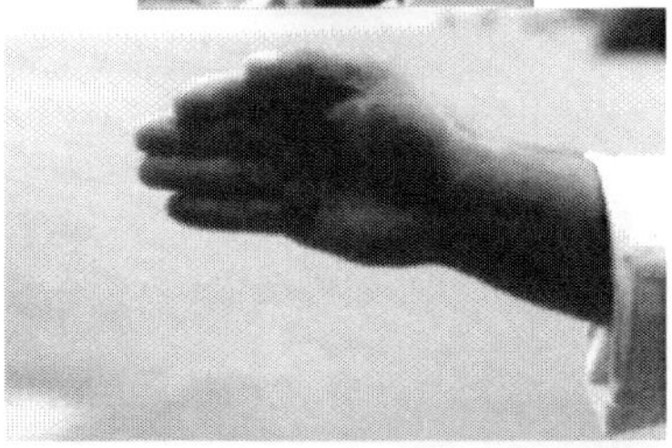

10. YOHON-NUKITE (FOUR-FINGER HAND SPEAR)
Extend the fingers, tightly together. Make the back of your hand slightly round and hold the fingers in position by clamping the thumb tightly against the base of your index finger. Attack the solar plexus.

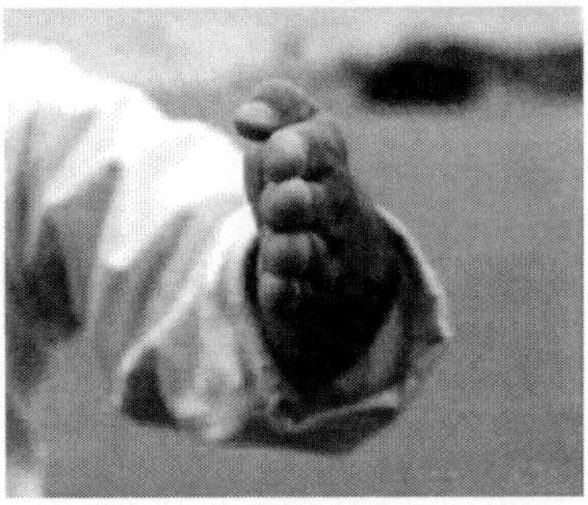

11. NIHON-NUKITE (TWO-FINGER HAND SPEAR)
Extend the index and middle fingers and hold the ring finger and little finger bent inside with the thumb tightly clamped against them. Use to attack the eyes.

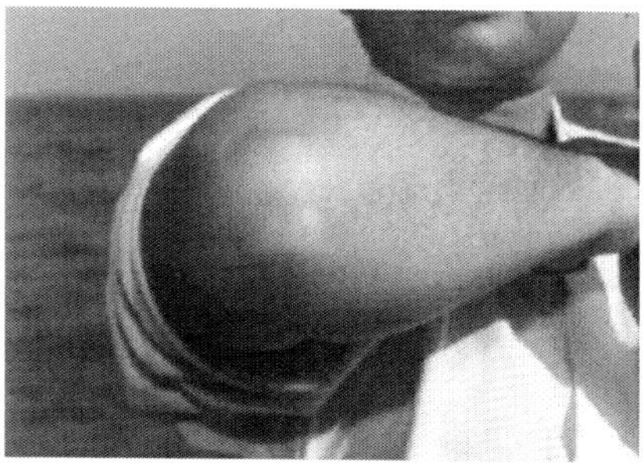

12. ENPI (ELBOW)
This is used to attack the lower jaw or the body, as well as to defend against an opponent's punch or kick. This is especially effective when your opponent is close. Even a frail woman or a child can use an elbow effectively.

13. GAIWANTO (OUTER ARM KNIFE) AND NAIWANTO (INNER ARM KNIFE)

Gaiwanto – The outer edge of your forearm, between the wrist and elbow, can be used to attack.

Naiwanto – The inner edge of the forearm. Both of these are used to defend against punches or kicks. Use the area near the wrist.

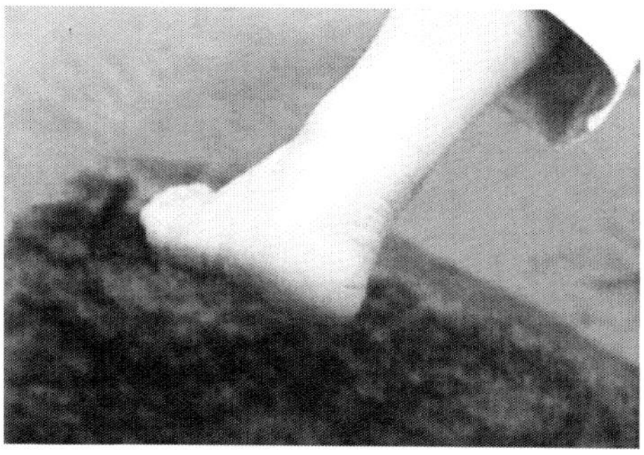

14. FEET AND LEGS
A. Sokuto (Knife-foot) Use the outer edge of your foot between the base of the little toe and the heel. This is used to kick sideward (high, middle, and low), or to simply kick in or kick up.

B. Tsumasaki (Sole) Use the ball of the foot at the base of the toes, while holding the toes curled upward. This is used for a front kick (high, middle, or low) or for a roundhouse kick.

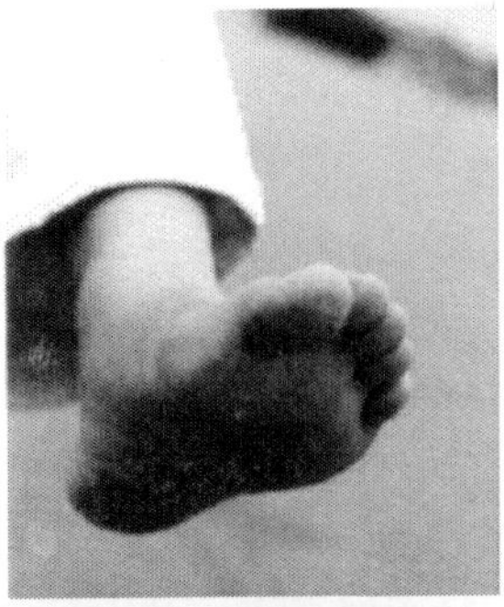

C. Kakato (Heel) The heel is used for stamping down, or for ushirogeri (Backward kick), usiromawashi (Backward kick where the foot is pivoted about the knee joint) or ushiro-mikazuki (a backward half-moon kick).

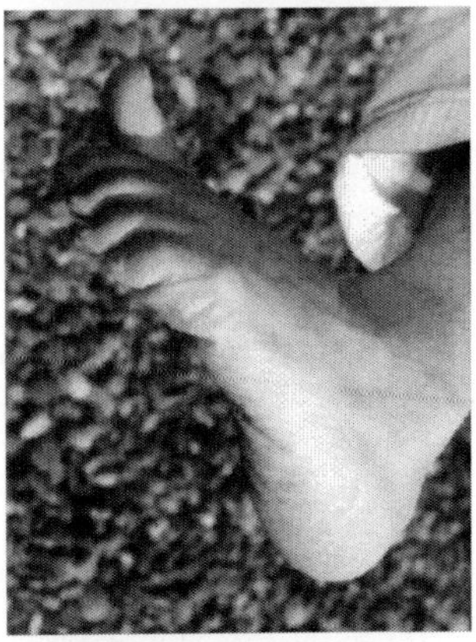

D. Hiza (Knee) The knee can be used to attack the assailant's groin and face.

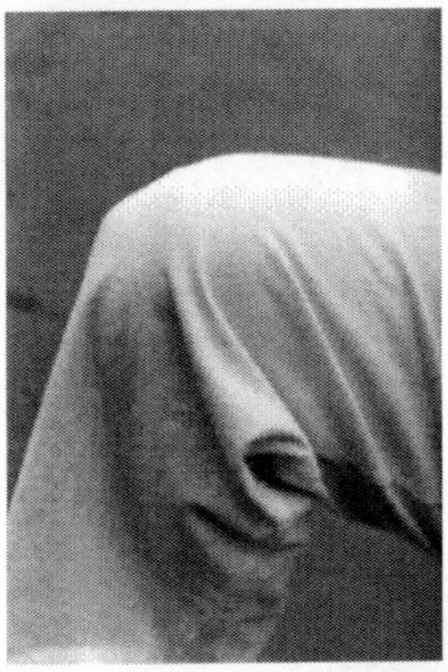

E. Sokko (Instep)
Hold the foot with the toes curled down and attack the assailant's groin with the instep. To kick, relax your ankle and use a snapping motion.

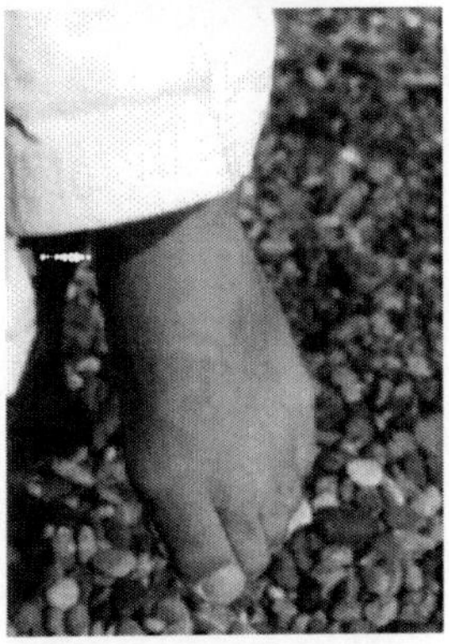

CHAPTER 2
STANCES

1. HEISOKUDACHI (CLOSED STANCE)

(1) Keep the heels and toes of both feet close together. Loosen the shoulders and elbows, close your hands lightly and hold the fists straight downward.

(2) Try to concentrate your entire body-strength in the stomach.

(3) Keep your eyes looking straight ahead. Draw your chin in and keep the upper part of your body from leaning to one side.

2. SHIZENTAI (NATURAL STANCE)

This is the natural standing position from which you can readily move into action either for attack or defense.

(1) Keep your feet shoulder-width apart.

(2) Relax the shoulders, keep the elbows flexible, hold the fists lightly hanging downward, and keep your natural stance.

(3) Place your body weight evenly on your two legs. Concentrate the whole strength of your body in the stomach.

(4) Don't tilt your head. Keep your chin pulled in and look straight ahead.

3. KIBADACHI (HORSE-RIDING STANCE)

(1) Open your legs to about twice shoulder-width (about 32 inches depending on your stature) and bend your knees, with the toes pulled inside of the heels. Push the knees outward so as to lower your waist.

(2) In lowering your waist, hold the upper part of your body straight, with the abdomen pushed forward. Place the center of your body weight as low as possible in order to concentrate your whole strength in the body center.

(3) For this stance, you should contract the anal muscle and concentrate the entire strength of your legs on the inside regions of the legs.

While practicing, always push the knees out but at the same time keep the toes pointing slightly inwards. Avoid a swaying movement as you go from one stance to the next; in other words, keep the weight of your body equally distributed and your center of gravity in the same horizontal plane.

4. ZENKUTSUDACHI (STANDING WITH THE FRONT LEG BENT – FRONT STANCE)

(1) Open your legs wide longitudinally (about 80 centimeters/32 inches depending on your stature) and bend the knee of your front leg almost to a right angle (90 degrees)

(2) Extend the rear leg straight.

(3) The 'sidewise' distance between your two legs should be shoulder-width. Your weight should be placed at the center of your body.
(4) The toes of the front foot should be turned slightly inward, while the toes of the rear foot should point straight forward.
(5) Stand with the front and rear legs drawn slightly toward each other. Firmly contract the muscles of the thighs and calves.

The front knee should be bent deeply and the rear leg extended straight simultaneously. Be sure to hold a firm stance.

5. KOKUTSUDACHI (BACK STANCE)

(1) Turn one foot (rear) toward the outside, with the other foot (front) facing straight forward to form a 'T' shape. Then, while maintaining this 'T' shape position, open the legs so that there is a distance of about 75 centimeters (30 inches) between the toes of the front foot and the heel of the rear foot. Bend the knees of both legs.

(2) Place 70% of your body weight on the rear foot and 30% on the front foot raising the heel of the front foot slightly off the ground. The knee of the rear leg should be kept bent outward.

(3) Your body should then be facing your opponent at an angle. This is a difficult way of standing, but it will help increase the resiliency and strength of your legs and waist. Standing in this position is in itself a good way to practice. Try to improve this stance using mirrors.

6. FUDO-DACHI (IMMOBILE STANCE)

(1) This stance is in between Kibadachi and Zenkutsudachi.

(2) From the Kibadachi stance, pivot one foot by 90 degrees and face in the direction of that foot. Bend your front leg deeply, while holding the rear leg's knee bent outward. At this time, be sure not to allow your body to shake.

(3) As a general feeling, try to push both knees away from one another.

This stance is often used in sparring. It is a firm and steady posture for standing and should be practiced until it seems natural. Keep your back straight at all times. Keeping your abdomen taut, pull your arms forward.

7. NEKOASHIDACHI (CAT STANCE)

This position resembles the posture of a cat ready to pounce upon its prey. *Since there is no weight on the front leg it is entirely free for kicking.*

Place your entire body weight on your rear leg. Bend the knee of the rear leg and the knee of the front leg with the toes of the front foot touching the ground lightly.

Keep the back straight in a line parallel with the hips.

While practicing, continually apply the basic principles to all your stances. Work hard to improve balance and stability; keep the back straight with the body and waist at the correct angle to your opponent. Check your posture continually, using a mirror when possible, and train with a partner who can correct you.

CHAPTER 3
HOW TO MOVE YOUR FEET AND LEGS

1. Zenkutsudachi (Front stance)

Take a left front stance.
Keep your back straight.

While holding your front leg steady, advance the rear foot by one step. It should move on a straight line toward the front foot, shortening the distance between both feet.

When your rear foot is even with the front, move it forcefully forward and to the right, to form a right front stance.

The front knee must be bent deeply, and the rear leg extended straight.

2. Kokutsudachi (Back stance)

Start in a right back stance (right leg forward).

Move your rear foot forward as close to your front as possible as you twist your body.

As your rear foot passes and becomes the front foot, you will have formed a new back stance.

Repeat both sides.

Keep 70% of your weight on the back leg. Keep your front hip tucked in.
Maintain an angle, which makes it harder to hit you.

3. Kibadachi (Horse-riding stance)
Assume a horse stance.

Move your right foot in front of your left. Keep your feet close together and your knees tight.

Repeat both sides.

Move your left foot to the left to form a new horse stance.

Repeat for both sides.

For a strong horse stance, push your knees out but keep your toes turned slightly inwards. Plant firmly and don't sway as you move.

4. Fudodachi (Immobile stance)

Place your right foot forward forming a half-moon position.

Bring your rear foot up to the center.

At the same time, pull your right arm back and left arm forward.

Slide your left foot forward to form a new fudo-dachi.

Repeat both sides.

Keep your back straight, and your stomach tight.

5. Nekoashidachi (Cat stance)

Bring your right foot forward with a half-moon sweep from inside to outside, moving as if to cover the groin area.

Front View

Side View

Keep your back in a straight line, parallel with your hips.

CHAPTER 4
HAND TECHNIQUES

HOW TO ATTACK

1. CHOKUZUKI (STRAIGHT PUNCH) from Natural Stance

(1) Assume a Shizentai or natural standing position.

(2) Place your left fist in front of the solar plexus, and put your right fist against the side of your body with the back of the right fist facing downward.

(3) Push your right fist forward, twisting it at the point of focus. Be sure not to let your right elbow swing out from your body. At the same time, draw back your left fist with your full strength, to a point above the left hip. Alternate right and left.

When you punch, extend your wrist straight forward so that the underarm muscle will become tight. Do not put too much tension in your shoulders at the instance you focus your punch. The center of your strength should be in your stomach.

2. CHOKUZUKI (STRAIGHT PUNCH) from Kibadachi

(1) Stand with legs apart and bent at the knee with the right arm extended and the fist clenched, fingers facing down.

(2) Rotate the right wrist 45 degrees clockwise.

(3) At the same time, bring the right arm back and the left forward.

(4) Complete the motion by extending the left arm completely forward and the right back.

3. GYAKUZUKI (REVERSE PUNCH)

(1) The right leg is back, the right arm extended forward.

(2) Bring the right leg forward, assuming the Zenkutsu-dachi stance.

(3) The right leg is brought forward swiveling from the hip.

(4) Counter-punch.

4. OIZUKI (Straight Punch with follow-up motion of the legs)

(1) From a natural standing position, push your left foot forward by one step to form the left-hand Gedanbarai position (i.e., bend the front leg deeply and extend the rear leg as straight as possible). Refer to the paragraph on Gedanbarai.

(2) Then, advance your rear (right) foot forward until it is level with the front foot. At this time, be sure to hold your back straight and to keep your right-hand fist firmly placed on the side of your body. While moving, your knee, torso, and head should be kept at the same level as for a left-hand Gedanbarai. Keep your eyes focused straight ahead.

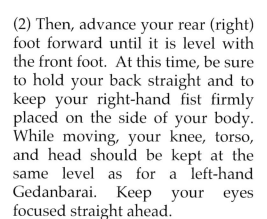

(2) Then, move your right foot forward to form a Zenkutsudachi stance at the same time punching with your right fist against the center or upper body of your opponent. Simultaneously, draw your left fist to your side just above the waistline with full power. Punch alternately right and left.

Once you feel comfortable with this technique, make the above-described motions without stopping. Concentrate on fluidity and speed.

HOW TO DEFEND

5. GEDAN BARAI I (DOWN BLOCK))

Analysis of the upper half of the body only

(1) In a natural stance, raise your left fist up to your right ear.

(2) Sweep the forearm downward forcefully, twisting it on the way.

(4) At the instant of blocking, the back of your hand should be facing upward. Your body should be in a half front-facing position. Repeat this motion alternately, right and left.

This technique should be practiced continually until it becomes second nature, as it is in constant use in all aspects of karate.

6. GEDAN BARAI II (LOWER BODY MOVEMENT)

(1) From a natural standing position, raise your left fist up to your right ear.

(2) Take a Zenkutsudachi stance while blocking with your left fist to fend off your opponent's attack (down-sweeping motion). Your body should be facing half-front. Your pulling hand should end up pressed against the right side of your body.

(3) In the down-sweeping motion, your fist should end up about three inches above your left knee.

(4) Next, bring your rear (right) foot up to the front foot, at the same time raising your right fist to your left ear. Do not raise or lower your body; your body should be kept at the same level.

(5) Repeat alternately, right and left. Follow the same instructions as for an Oizuki punch. Be sure not to let your rear heel come off the ground. Have your rear leg extended straight. Your feet should always be in contact with the floor. *Do not lean forward. Keep your eyes straight ahead.*

7. GEDAN-BARAI III (HOW TO TURN YOUR BODY)

(1) Facing away, with right leg forward. Preparing to turn and use the right hand. (Left-hand orientation can be made by reversing the instructions).

(2) As you turn your head to the rear, move your rear foot as shown in the picture.

(3) Then turn your torso and at the same time execute a Gedanbarai (down-fending-off action).

(4) Execute an Oizuki punch and move forward. *Move quickly while holding your stance firm and stable.*

8. AGE-UKE (RISING BLOCK) I

The Age-Uke is used to block an attack to your face.

(1) From a natural standing position, bring your left fist back against the left side of your waist and place your right hand (with the palm open) in front of the upper part of your body.

(2) Swing your left arm upward, crossing it outside of your right hand.

Front view *Side View*

(3) At the same time, pull your right fist back to the side of your body.

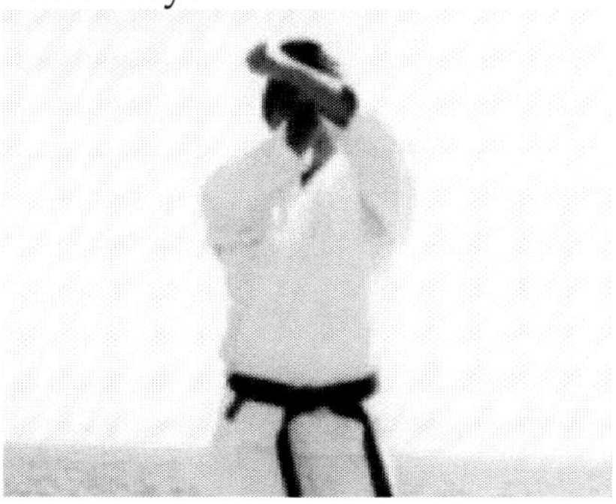

In blocking an attack, try to take full advantage of the power of your elbow by making it snap up. The body should be twisted away from the block to an angle of approximately 45 degrees.

9. AGE-UKE (RISING BLOCK) II

(1) Make a left hand Age-Uke from a natural standing position.

(2) Move your left hand up and inward as if to draw a semi-circle and place it in front of your forehead. Draw your right hand back.

(3) Keep your right fist pressed against your waist. (By opening your hand you could grasp your assailant's arm and draw it toward yourself).

(3) To continue to the other side, draw your rear foot up.

(4) Move your right (rear) foot one step forward to form a Zenkutsudachi stance and at the same time cross your right hand under your left hand and snap your elbow up to block your assailant's attack.

(4) At the same time pull your left hand (clenched in a fist) to the left side of your waist.

(5) Complete the block.

Perform this motion alternately right and left. Be sure to hold your elbow, waist, and rear foot on a straight line.

10. CHUDAN-SOTO-UKE (OUTSIDE BLOCK) I

For defending (and attacking) the midsection.

(1) Assume a natural standing position.

(2) Extend your right hand in front of your solar plexus and bring your left forefist over your head as shown in the picture.

(3) Twist the left fist as you swing it down.

(4) Pull your right hand back toward the right side of your waist.

Keep your wrist extended and straight. Your body and the arm of your blocking hand should be a fist's width apart. The fist of your blocking hand should be at shoulder level.

11. CHUDAN-SOTO-UKE (OUTSIDE BLOCK) II

(1) Take a natural standing position.

(2) Take a left front stance, raise your left fist up above your head, and swing it down to block a midlevel attack. Pull your right hand back against your waist.

(3) Move your right foot one step forward, at the same time raising your right hand over your head.

(4) Form a front stance and swing your right hand downward down to block an attack to your midsection. Pull your left hand back against your waist. Your body should be half-front facing.

(5) Repeat alternately right and left. The general idea is the same as for Gedanbarai and Age-Uke

12. CHUDAN-UCHI-UKE (INSIDE BLOCK) I

For defending and attacking to the midsection.

(1) In a natural stance, extend your right hand in front of your solar plexus and invert left fist against the right side of your body.

(2) Twist your left fist as you block. Hold your fist lightly at the beginning, and then tighten it up at the instant of blocking. Bend your elbow fully.

13. CHUDAN-UCHI-UKE (INSIDE BLOCK) II

(1) Take a natural standing position.

(2) Form a Zenkutsudachi stance by moving your left foot one step forward, and at the same time, perform a left-hand Chudan-Uchi-Uke (inside-block to the midsection).

(3) While moving your right foot one step forward, bring your right fist under your left armpit.

(4) Then, while forming a Zenkutsudachi stance, block the attack to your midsection with your right fist. Pull your left fist back against the left side of your body.
(5) Repeat right and left.

14. SHUTO-UKE (KNIFE-HAND BLOCK) I

(1) From a natural stance, raise your left knife-hand up to your right ear, with the thumb-side up, stretch your right knife-hand forward in front of your solar plexus (with the back facing up).

(2) Twist your wrist as you sweep down with your left hand.

(3) Bend your elbow fully and keep the knife-hand, wrist, and elbow on a straight line. Hold your fingertips at the same level as your shoulders. Bend your thumb slightly and keep it forced tightly against your hands. Your pulling hand should end up pressed against your solar plexus, ready for a spear-hand attack.

15. SHUTO-UKE (KNIFE-HAND BLOCK) II

(1) From the natural standing position, move your right foot back by one step and execute a left knife-hand block in a Kokutsu-dachi (back stance).

(2) As you move, your right hand should be pulled back against your solar plexus.

(3) Then, move your rear (right) foot forward by one step, at the same time bringing your right knife-hand up to your left ear.

(4) As soon as you form the Kokutsudachi stance, block your assailant's attack with your right knife-hand. Pull your left knife-hand back against your solar plexus.

(5) Perform this motion alternately right and left.

16. FUDODACHI-GYAKUZUKI

(1) Fudo-dachi.

(2) Bring the right leg forward.

(3) Step into a Fudo-dachi.

(4) Assuming a firm stance, counter-punch with the left arm.

17. SHUTO-UKE IN NEKOASHIDASHI (CAT STANCE)

(1) Stand with left leg forward, left arm also extended forward and bent at a 90-degree angle at the elbow.

(2) Extend the right arm forward at shoulder height, fingers unclenched. The right leg, knee bent, also comes forward.

(3) The right arm sweeps across the body to the left as if to grasp the opponent's arm.

(4) The right elbow is bent and brought in to the body.

18. SHUTO-UCHI (KNIFE-HAND STRIKE)

(1) From a natural standing position, extend your left hand (open)

(3) Raise your left arm, palm forward, forming a knife-hand with your right hand.

(4) Step forward with your left leg into a front stance.

(4) Simultaneously twist your arm and strike the opponent's neck with your knife-hand, while at the same time withdrawing your right hand. The overall movement is similar to that of an outside arm block.

19. SHUTO-USHIRO MAMASHI-UCHI (SPINNING KNIFE-HAND)

(1) Assume a right horse stance (right leg forward, with both hands in blocking position across your body, left hand above right).

(2) Execute a knife-hand strike with your right hand.

(3) Spin around behind you to the left (left leg leading) towards your opponent to form a left horse stance.

(4) Strike your opponent's neck with your left knife-hand.

20. HAITO-UCHI (RIDGE-HAND STRIKE)

(1) Assume a left-leg forward front stance and left downblock, with your right hand inverted at your hip.

(2) Step forward into a right front stance. As you do so form a knife-hand with your inverted right hand. Snap your right hand forward and strike your opponent's neck or head with the ridge (thumb-side) of your right hand (be careful to properly tuck your thumb over your palm). Simultaneously withdraw your left hand.

This technique can form a counter-strike, similar to a counter-punch, when used immediately following a block without stepping forward.

21. URAKEN (BACK-FIST STRIKE)

(1) From a right-leg forward stance, reach across your body with your right hand.

(2) Backfist with your right fist. Immediately withdraw your striking hand.

22. MAWASHI URAKEN (SPINNING BACK-FIST)

(1) Assume a left horse stance, with both hands in blocking position across your body.

(2) Step around behind, right leg first, towards your opponent to form a right horse stance.
(3) Strike with the back of your right fist.
(4) Immediately snap back to blocking position.

23. UCHI-ORASHI-URAKEN (BACK-FIST AGAINST KICK)

(1) From a natural stance, as opponent kicks, step forward with your right leg and strike down on his instep with a right back-fist.

(2) Depending on distance, this technique is an effective counter to a kick with or without stepping, and may be used to augment body shifting to avoid the incoming kick.

24. GYAKU-URA-KEN (REVERSE-BACK-FIST)

(1) From a natural stance, step forward with your left leg into a fighting stance.

(2) Strike your opponent's head or neck with a left hand reverse back fist.

25. TEISHO-UCHI (PALM-HEEL STRIKE)

(1) From a natural stance, step forward and execute a left downblock.

(2) Form a palm heel with your right hand. To do this, close your thumb as in a knife-hand. Roll your fingers closed to the second digit only rather than forming a complete fist.

(2) Strike with your right hand, tilting your hand backwards so that you connect with the heel of your right palm.

(3) Depending upon distance, you could step forward while executing this strike.

26. BREATHING

(1) How to perform deep breathing.

a. Inhale air quietly and deeply through your nose (for about seven seconds).

b. Send the air to the chest and abdomen and fill them up (for about three seconds).

c. Breathe out through the nose about 70% of the air inhaled (for about ten seconds).

d. Stop breathing, leaving some air still inside (about three seconds).

Repeat these steps.

(2) How to breathe while exercising.

Breathe according to the rhythm of your body movements. For practice:

a. Inhale short and exhale short.

b. Inhale long and exhale long.

c. Inhale long and exhale short.

These three steps should be practiced repeatedly until you become able to maintain quiet and orderly breathing all the time.

(3) Breathing practice with downward block.

a. Take a natural standing position.

b. Inhale deeply through your nose.

c. Send the air to your abdomen and hold it there.

d. Step forward with your left foot and execute a left-hand downward block. At the same time exhale sharply.

(4) Breathing with offensive and defensive techniques.

In karate, inhale on the defensive and exhale on the offensive. Inhale quietly, gradually, and continuously through the nose so that your opponent can't detect it. Exhale nasally in time with your opponent's movements. If breathing is interrupted or out of time, exhale through your mouth to regain the proper harmony. Focus your concentration in the abdomen. Tighten the sphincter muscle while inhaling and relax it while exhaling. Remain calm throughout.

CHAPTER 5
FOOT TECHNIQUES

1. MAE-GERI (Front Kick)

(1) Take a Zenkutsudachi. Clench your fists in freestyle position.

(2) While shifting your body weight to the front foot, bring your rear foot forward and raise it toward your chest.

(3) Then, snapping your knee, kick out against the target.

(4) As soon as the kick is completed draw the kicking foot back to its original position and return to the Zenkutsudachi position. Alternatively, one could step forward instead of withdrawing the leg. Practice both sides. Also practice from a natural stance.
Snap back the foot quickly, as soon after the kick as possible. Otherwise, it might be caught by your opponent.

3. MAE-MAWASHI GERI (Roundhouse Kick)

(1) Assume a Zenkutsudachi standing position.

(2) Lift your kicking leg up sideways, to a horizontal position.

(3) While turning around your waist, draw a semi-circle with your foot, around the knee, and hit the target at a right angle (while making sure to hold a firm stance with your standing leg).

(4) After kicking, draw the foot back quickly, as in the case of a Maegeri (Front Kick).

4. MIKAZUKI-GERI (Crescent Kick)

This kick uses the sole of the foot to block an assailant's mid-level punch or attacking your enemy's abdomen, groin, etc.

(1) From a Kibadachi (horse-riding) stance extend your left hand outward with the elbow slightly bent.

(2) While shifting your body weight over the left foot, swing your right foot around in a crescent motion.

(3) The striking surface is the sole of the foot.

(4) After kicking, pull your kicking foot back and resume the Kibadachi stance. Repeat alternately right and left.

This kick may be practiced by striking the left hand, which is held fully extended from your side.

5. YOKOGERI (Side Thrust Kick) I

(1) Take a closed-stance position.

(2) Raise your left knee to your chest and place your body weight on your right foot. Turn your face to the left.

(3) Then, kick out your left foot against the target. Push out your heel first. Hold a firm stance while kicking.

(4) After kicking, pull your foot back the return to closed stance.

Use the outer edge of your foot between the base of the little toe and the heel. This is used to kick sideways (high, middle and low) or simply to kick in or up.

6. YOKOGERI (Side Thrust Kick) II

(1) From a natural stance, draw your right foot back by one step to form a Kibadachi (horse-riding) stance, and at the same time, turn your face to the left. Place your right fist lightly over your solar plexus, and extend your left fist in the direction of your movement.

(2) Draw your rear (right) foot one step forward, crossing it in front of your front (left) foot. Shift your body weight onto your left foot. Keep your back straight.

(3) Raise your left knee to your chest.

4) Push your heel out first and hit the target with the edge of your foot. Concentrate your body weight onto your kicking foot as it hits the target.

(5) Using the reaction force of the kicking foot, bring your knee back to your chest, returning to position 3 above.

(6) Then, resume your Kibadachi position. Take the same procedures for either forward or backward movement. Repeat alternately right and left.

Be sure to have the foot move on a straight line. Keep your eyes watching the target. Make a distinction in kicking upper, middle, and lower targets. This is a difficult kick and requires extensive practice. Once mastered, it is very powerful.

<u>7. YOKOGERI (in Kekomi form, Side Thrust Kick) III</u>
(1) KIBADACHI

(2) Raise your left knee towards your chest.

(3) Twist your standing foot halfway around, while keeping your left knee raised.

(4) Then, thrust your knife-foot against the target. After kicking, pull your leg back and resume the Kibadachi stance.

8. KEAGE (Side Snap Kick)

For Keage the knee points diagonally towards the target. It looks the same as a Kekomi, however, at the moment of impact.

(1) Take a Kibadachi (horse-stance) position.

(2) Raise your left knee and point it towards the target.

(3) Execute the kick using the snapping force of the knee.

(4) Withdraw your leg immediately and return to kibadachi.

This kick is useful for both blocking and attacking.

9. USHIRO-GERI or UMA-GERI (Back Kick) I

(1) Take a natural standing position.

(2) As in the front kick, hold the knee of your kicking leg up toward your chest. Look in the direction in which you are to kick.

(3) While leaning your upper body forward, thrust the heel of your kicking foot backwards, against the target. Return to natural stance

This is useful when you are attacked from behind. This kick is powerful, but care should be taken in order to make it a timely kick, for an attack from behind is usually made unexpectedly.

10. USHIRO-GERI (Back Kick) II

(1) Take a slightly tilted Zenkutsudachi standing position, with the feet drawn closer to each other than usual. This should make it possible to move your waist around swiftly.

(2) Turn your front ankle around so the heel faces towards the target. As soon as you turn around, bring your kicking foot close to your standing foot. Your head should be turned to look at the target.

(3) Quickly raise your kicking leg.

(5) Then, thrust out your kicking foot, with its side almost rubbing the side of your other leg.

(6) After kicking, pull your leg back and resume your original posture.

In backward kicking, you are apt to make yourself unguarded at the moment of kicking; be sure to move as swiftly as possible!

11. GYAKU-MIKAZUKI-GERI (Hook Kick)

This is used to attack your assailant's face and abdomen from the side. This is a highly specialized technique and difficult to master.

(1) From a natural standing position, draw your right foot backwards and form a kibadachi right stance.

(2) Cross your right foot behind the left foot facing the left heel towards the target. Your body is positioned slightly backwards away from your target.

(3) Move your body weight over the right foot and turn your waist around halfway and at the same time swing the heel of your left foot around in a crescent motion.

(4) Put down your kicking foot in front of you and resume the zenkutsudachi stance (or kibadachi).

To get the general feeling, pivot yourself around your waist, and move your heel at the moment of kicking as if to hook the target, while placing all of your body weight on the back leg. Since it is difficult to coordinate the movement of the kicking foot, the waist, and the upper body all into one motion, much practice is required to master this kick.

12. USHIRO-MAWASHI-GERI (Backward Revolving Kick)

This is a technique intended to take full advantage of centrifugal force. It is a mixture between a back kick and a reverse crescent kick and is useful to attack an assailant's face.

(1) Assume a tilted zenkutsudachi posture with the stance closer than usual.

(2) Turn your front foot around so that the heel faces the target and at the same time draw the rear foot quickly toward the front foot. Your upper body will be turned backward.

(3) – (5) While twisting your waist around as in the case of a crescent kick,
kick out with your heel against the target. Try to move it so as to describe a circle the highest point of which is the point of contact. By bringing your kicking foot around the foot will be returned to the starting position after drawing a full circle in the air.

This kick can be likened to whirling a string with a weight tied to it. Here, the heel is a weight, the leg is a piece of string, and the center of the revolving motion is your waist. This technique requires much practice to master.

13. COMBINATION KICK EXERCISE (Front, side, round and back kicks on one leg)

As well as helping to develop effective kicking of two or more opponents that have surrounded you, this is a very useful training exercise for balance and kicking poise.

(1) From a right front stance, execute a right front kick

(2) Snap your leg back but do not lower it. Execute a side thrust kick to your right.

(3) Snap your leg back, but do not lower it. Execute a right-leg round kick to the front.

(4) Snap your leg back, but do not lower it. Execute a right-leg back kick to the rear.

(5) Snap your leg back, but do not lower it. Return to your initial stance, and alternate legs.

CHAPTER 6
JUMPING KICK TECHNIQUES

1. NIDAN-GERI (Two-Step Jumping Kick)

(1) Take either a Zenkutsudachi or Nekoashidachi (Cat Stance) position.

(2) Front kick with your rear leg

(3) Jump off the ground by pushing down forcibly with your kicking leg.

(3) Before the foot gets back to the ground, front kick with your other leg, making use of the reaction force of the first kick.

In making the first kick, make the best use of the snapping force, and then try to make the second kick as forcefully as possible. This is a technique to make two kicks in one jump. Be sure not to let your opponent find any opening for attack, especially at the moment you hit the ground.

2. FLYING FRONT ROUND HOUSE KICK

Jump off the ground by pushing off with your front leg while raising your rear knee. Quickly twist your body and execute a roundhouse kick with your front leg.

3. TOBIYOKO-GERI (Jumping Side Kick)

(1) Jump off the ground by pushing down on the ground forcibly with your left foot.

(2) The moment after jumping, hold your left leg close to your body, and at the same time thrust out your right leg attacking your target.

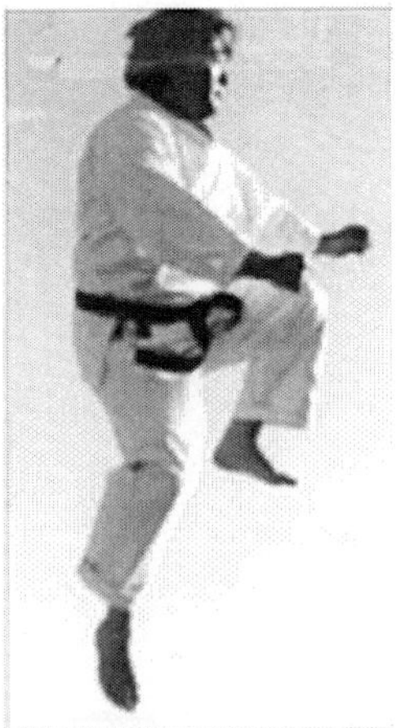

Extend the knee of the kicking leg forcefully, and push out the knife-foot with the heel turned somewhat upward. The instant of kicking, make the kicking leg draw a downward line against the target, while concentrating your body weight onto the edge of the knife foot.

4. TOBI-USHIRO-GERI (Backward Jumping Kick)

(1) Assume a Zenkutsudachi or sparring stance. Jump off the ground by forcibly pushing down on the ground with your front foot.

(2) The instant of jumping, twist your body around halfway, centering around your front foot, with the rear leg protecting your body from your assailant.

(3) The moment you finish turning, make a backward kick with your left foot, utilizing your turning motion.

It is important to make the semicircle as small as possible, and to move as swiftly as possible.

5. TOBI-USHIRO-MAWASHI (Jumping Back Roundhouse Kick)

Jump off the ground and turn halfway around up in the air, just like for a 'tobi-ushiro-geri,' and at the final stage of turning, execute an 'ushiro-mawashi' (backward revolving kick).

6. TOBI-GAKU-MIKAZUKI-GERI (Flying Hook Kick)

Jump off the ground and swing the heel of your right foot in a crescent motion, just as for a Gaku-mikazuki-geri (Hook Kick).

7. FLYING SCISSORS KICK

(1) Right-footed flying hook kick.

(2) Immediately twist your body and execute a flying back roundhouse kick.

CHAPTER 7
Makiwara (Punching Board) Exercises

HOW TO PRACTICE ON THE MAKIWARA

Pay close attention to the movements of your shoulders and waist, and make your punch, strike, or kick as forceful as possible. Every practice should be carried out in earnest. To practice every day is the best way to attain mastery.

Repeated daily practice by thrusting or kicking against the makiwara will turn the plain hands or feet into really powerful and destructive weapons. The art of breaking tiles, bricks, or boards owes largely to the training with sheaved straws.

It is most important to design the training methods so as to fit one's own physical situation and to continue the practice every day. *Start slowly in practicing these training techniques, gradually building up power and speed.*

A. SEIKEN (FOREFIST) Execute a reverse punch

1. When the punch is made, be sure not to raise the shoulder on the side of the punching arm.

2. Don't bend your rear leg, or raise your head.
3. Pull back as quickly as possible.

B. ENPI (ELBOW)

1. Stand closer to the straw bundle than for a seiken. Turn your waist sufficiently to enable you to hit the straw with your elbow.

2. In making the punch, place your body weight forcefully onto your front knee. Pull back your arm quickly to your waist.

C. SHUTO (KNIFE-HAND)

1. Take a Kibadachi stance.

2. Raise your knife-hand over your head, and swing it down to hit the target with a part of the knife-hand near the wrist.

3. At the moment of hitting, be sure to hold the elbow firm and tight. The idea is the same as for tettsui (hammer-fist).

D. HAITO (Knife-hand)

1. Take a front stance

2. Draw your left hand to your opposite ear.

3. Strike the target with the knife-edge of your hand.

E. UCHI-UKE (INSIDE FOREARM BLOCK)

1. From a kibadachi stance, bring your blocking fist (left) under right armpit, at the same time extending right arm directly forward.

2. Strike the target with the inside of the left forearm, simultaneously pulling back the right fist to your waist.

F. OUTSIDE FOREARM BLOCK

1. Assume a kibadachi stance
2. Draw your right fist up and back.

3. Strike the target with the little finger-side of your inverted right fist.

G. URA-KEN(Backfist)

1. Take a kibadachi (horse-riding) stance.

2. As shown in the picture, bring your fist close to your ear, and hit the target.

3. Try to hit the target with the whole area of the back of your hand. Be sure to concentrate your body strength onto your hitting hand.

H. FRONT ROUND KICK

1. Assume a right front stance

2. Lift your left leg in preparation for round kick

3. Strike the target with the ball of your foot.

4. This kick may also be executed with the instep.

I. SIDE KICK

1. Assume a left kibadachi at one-step width away from the target

2. Step in with your right leg.

3. Strike the target with the knife-edge of your left leg.

CHAPTER 8
OTHER EXERCISES

1. Training with Weights

A. STRAIGHT PUNCH USING HAND WEIGHTS

These exercises are helpful in practicing basic punching and blocking movements. Try also with downward, inside, and outside blocks, starting slowly and gradually increasing speed as proficiency is attained.

B. STRAIGHT PUNCH WITH BAR BELL

By using leg weights, balance and strength may be considerably increased.

C. FRONT KICK EXERCISE

D. SIDE THRUST KICK EXERCISE

E. SQUAT KICK WITH BARBELL.

2. Effective methods of training for a team of two.

(1) USING KIBADACHI STANCE.

As shown in the picture, carry your partner on your shoulders. The carrying time may be short at the beginning, but as you become used to it, try to keep carrying for a much longer time. Tensing and relaxing of the legs and stomach muscles will also improve your stance.

(2) USING ZENKUTSUDACHI STANCE.

With a partner on your shoulders, execute a front kick. This method of training ensures the same height is maintained, and the back heel is kept firmly on the ground. A strong stance is necessary after the kick.

CHAPTER 9
UKEMI TECHNIQUES (Falling Safely)

This is the term used to denote various ways of falling without receiving any injuries, when one is thrown to the ground.

1. Koho-Ukemi (Backward Ukemi) I

Lie on your back, pull your chin in, raise your head, cross your arms and raise them up. Your eyes should be looking at your own belt. Press the fingers of the raised hands together. When the arms are extended, the hands should hit the ground, at the same time. The arms should be neither too far from nor too close to your body.

2. Koho-Ukemi II

Put both feet together and extend your legs. Then, from a sitting position, cross your arms and raise them up in front of you. Raise your legs and let the upper part of your body fall backwards. The instant your back touches the floor, hit the ground with your hands. As the next advanced step, you should practice learning this 'ukemi' using only one hand.

3. Koho-Ukemi III

Raise the heels of both feet, and bend your knees. Bring your hands in front of you. Roll your body backwards. The instant your back touches the ground, hit the ground with your hands. Roll back up and repeat.

4. Koho-Ukemi IV

From a standing position, bend your left knee and raise your right foot up in front of you, meanwhile raising your right hand in front of you. The next moment, throw yourself backward and make the 'ukemi' action with your right hand.

5. Zenpo-Ukemi (Forward Ukemi)

Put your right hand on the ground, with the fingertips bent inside, and roll forward by placing your right shoulder, waist, and left leg etc. smoothly on the ground. After a full rotation, make the 'ukemi' action with your left hand. As you became more experienced, try to place your hand at a point much farther away from yourself and still be able to make the 'ukemi' motion.

VOLUME III: Combination Techniques & Kumite Applications

CHAPTER 1
Fundamental Combination Techniques

1. Gedan-Barai and Chudan-Gyakuzuki
(Down-block and reverse punch to midsection)

1. Take a natural stance

2. Advance your left foot by one step into a front stance and downblock

3. Remaining in the same place, execute a right-side reverse punch, drawing your left fist firmly back to your side.

4. Repeat alternately left and right, moving forward and backward.

Your body should be at a 45° with respect to the front when you block, then twist fully forward when you punch. Drive your hip forcefully forward to propel your punch.

2. Gedan-Barai and Chudan-Gyakuzuki in Fudo-Dachi (Immovable stance)

The movements are the same as above for Zenkutsu-Dachi

3. Age-Uke and Gyakuzuki
(Rising block and reverse punch)

1. From a natural stance, advance your left foot by one step into either a front stance or fudo dachi and execute a rising block

2. Remaining in the same place, execute a right-side reverse punch, drawing your left fist firmly back to your side.

3. Repeat alternately left and right, moving forward and backward.

Your body should be at a 45° with respect to the front when you block, then twist fully forward when you punch. Drive your hip forcefully forward to propel your punch.

4. Chudan Soto-Uke and Gyakuzuki
(Outside block to midsection and reverse punch)

1. From a natural stance, advance your left foot by one step into either a front stance or fudo dachi and execute a mid-level outside block

2. Remaining in the same place, execute a right-side reverse punch, drawing your left fist firmly back to your side.

3. Repeat alternately left and right, moving forward and backward.

Your body should be at a 45° with respect to the front when you block, then twist fully forward when you punch. Drive your hip forcefully forward to propel your punch.

5. Chudan Uchi-Uke and Gyakuzuki (Inside block to midsection and reverse punch)

1. From a natural stance, advance your left foot by one step into either a front stance or fudo dachi and execute a mid-level inside block

2. Remaining in the same place, execute a right-side reverse punch, drawing your left fist firmly back to your side.

3. Repeat alternately left and right, moving forward and backward.

Your body should be at a 45° with respect to the front when you block, then twist fully forward when you punch. Drive your hip forcefully forward to propel your punch.

6. Shuto-Uke and Gyakuzuki in Fudodachi stance
(Knife-hand block, back stance, reverse punch in fudo dachi)

1. Take a natural stance

2. Advance your left foot by one step into a back stance and execute a mid-level knife-hand block

3. Shift your front leg across to form a fudo-dachi, while driving your rear hip forward and execute a right-side reverse punch, drawing your left fist firmly back to your side.

4. Repeat alternately left and right, moving forward and backward.

Use of a back stance while blocking places your body at a 45° with respect to the front, which protects you when you block. Twisting your hips forward in the fudo-dachi adds hip power to your punch.

7. JuJi-Uke (Crossed-hands block)

Jodan (upper) JuJi-Uke

As soon as you form a front stance, block your opponent's attack by crossing your arms in front of your forehead.

This is useful for blocking upper punches, and puts you in a position to grab your opponent's arm.

Gedan (Lower) JuJi-Uke

As above, but form fists and block low. This is useful for blocking your opponent's kicks.

8. Forward and Reverse Punches

1. Take a front stance or fudo dachi

2. Execute a forward jab
3. Follow immediately with a reverse punch to the midsection. Pull your jabbing hand back forcefully. Take care to twist your waist to drive your hip forward during the punch.
4. Punching hand should be withdrawn immediately, to return to fighting position.

9. Uraken and Gyakuzuki (Back fist and reverse punch)

1. From a natural stance, take a left-leg forward front stance or fudo-dachi and execute a left back fist.

2. Right hand reverse punch to the midsection.
3. Practice both sides

10. Uraken Mawashi-Uchi and Gyakuzuki (Spinning back fist and reverse punch)

1. Take a left-leg forward kibadachi (horse stance) with guarding hands

2. Spin around behind, land in a horse stance and execute a right back fist.

3. Immediately shift your front foot over to form a front stance or fudo-dachi and execute a reverse punch to the midsection. Immediately shift your front foot over to form a front stance or fudo-dachi and execute a reverse punch to the midsection.

4. Practice both sides.

11. Uchi Oroshi-Uraken and Gyakuzuki
(Back fist to a kicking leg and reverse punch)

1. From a natural stance, step forward with your right leg into a front stance or fudo-dachi. Simultaneously raise your right fist in a high arc.

2. Strike down forcefully with a backfist onto the toes of a kicking leg.

3. Follow with a mid-level reverse punch.

12. Gyuku Uraken and Gyakuzuki (Outside back fist and reverse punch)

1. From a natural stance, step into a left front stance or fudo-dachi. Strike the side of your opponent's head with an outside backfist.

2. Follow with a right reverse punch

3. Practice both sides.

13. Shuto-Uchi and Gyakuzuki

1. From a natural stance, step into a right front stance or fudo-dachi and strike your opponent's head or neck with the knife-edge of your right hand.

2.Follow with a left reverse punch.

3. Practice both sides.

14. Haito and Gyakuzuki

1. From a natural stance, step into a left front stance or fudo-dachi and strike your opponent's head or neck with the thumb side of your left hand. Form a strong knife-hand.

2. Follow with a right reverse punch.

3. Practice both sides.

15. Ushiro Shuto Mawashi-Uchi and Gyakuzuki (Spinning back fist and reverse punch)

1. From a natural stance, step into a left front stance or fudo-dachi with guarding hands

3. Spin around behind, land in a right front stance and execute a right knife-hand strike to the head or neck.
4. Follow with a left reverse punch to the midsection.
5. Practice both sides

16. Gedan barai and Teisho (Down block and palm-heel strike)

1. From a natural stance, step into a left front stance or fudo-dachi and execute a down block.

2. Strike your opponent with the palm-heel of your right hand. Twist your hip forward as in a reverse punch.

3. Practice both sides.

CHAPTER 2
Advanced Combination Techniques

1. Half-step jab and reverse punch

1. Sparring stance

2. Pull the rear foot up a half-step.

3. Jab with the front hand

4. Reverse punch.

5. Return immediately to sparring position

2. Half-step knee up jab and reverse punch

1. Sparring stance

2. Pull the rear foot up a half-step.

3. Lift your front knee to hip height and jab with the front hand.

4. Reverse punch. Lower your stance for maximum power.

3. Half-step knee up back fist and reverse punch

1. Sparring stance

2. Pull the rear foot up a half-step.

3. Lift your front knee to hip height and back fist with the front hand

4. Reverse Punch

4. Jab, stepping punch and reverse punch

1. Sparring stance

2. Jab with the front hand (You can pull the rear foot up a half-step depending upon distance).

3. Stepping punch

4. Reverse Punch

5. Knee-up stepping punch and reverse punch

1. Sparring stance

2. Bring your rear knee up as if to execute a front kick.

3. Continue moving the rear leg forward to complete a stepping punch.

4. Reverse punch. Lower your stance for maximum power.

6. Jab, reverse punch and front kick

1. Sparring stance

2. Jab with the front hand.
3. Reverse punch.
4. Front kick

7. Jab, reverse punch and front leg front kick

1. Sparring stance

2. Jab with the front hand.

3. Reverse punch

4. Draw your rear leg up and front kick with your front foot. This is useful to close distance.

8. Jab, reverse punch and roundhouse kick

1. Sparring stance

2. Jab with the front hand.

3. Reverse punch
4. Front roundhouse kick

9. Reverse sword-hand and spinning sword-hand

1. In a sparring stance, execute a haito with your front hand.

2. Spin around behind in a continuous movement in the direction of the haito.

3. Execute a shuto as you complete your turn into the opposite-die sparring stance.

10. Jab, reverse punch, side kick and back kick

1. Sparring stance

2. Jab with the front hand.

3. Reverse punch.

4. Bring your rear leg up and side kick

5. Place the kicking leg down, keeping your eye on your opponent

6. Spin around, sight your opponent quickly

7. Back kick

11. Front roundhouse kick, back roundhouse kick and front roundhouse kick

1. Sparring stance

2. Bring the rear leg forward and front roundhouse kick.

3. Place the leg in front.

4. While watching your opponent, continue spinning in the same direction and execute a back roundhouse (wheel) kick.

5. Lower your kicking leg in front to form a new sparring stance.

6. Execute another front roundhouse kick and step forward into a front stance.

12. Jab, reverse punch, hook kick and back roundhouse kick

1. Sparring stance

2. Jab with the front hand.

3. Reverse punch

4. Bring your rear leg across and execute a hook kick.

7. Place the kicking leg in front.

6. Keeping your eyes on your opponent, spin around in the opposite direction and execute a back roundhouse kick.

7. Bring your leg all the way back or place it forward, depending upon distance from your opponent.

CHAPTER 3
Introduction to Kumite

1. Significance of Kumite

Kumite practice is essential to develop timing, focus, distance and taisabaki. It is the integrated application of the various basic Karate techniques. You must take care not to become so engrossed in kumite practice that you neglect training in basics and kata. Basics, and combinations of basics, are the tools that are used in kumite. Kata demonstrates multiple applications of basics and combinations against opponents in all directions. The secret to excellence in kumite lies in basics and kata.

2. Rules for Kumite Practice

Always bow at the start and end of every kumite. Courtesy is the golden rule. Train in earnest, but control your techniques; do not allow yourself to get excited and hurt your opponents. Always maintain the conduct of a gentleman.

3. How to Practice Kumite

Always practice in earnest, giving the best training to each other. When assuming the offensive role, you must attack convincingly both for yourself and to spur on your opponent. Execute your attacks with sufficient energy that your opponent will feel that he will be hurt if he does not block or avoid them, otherwise neither of you will train correctly. When defending, consider that you must block or avoid the oncoming blow or you will be crushed. In this manner, you will develop the courage to deal with a real situation.

When you make a "kime" (winning attack, or decisive blow), make a "ki-ai" (shout) with all of your strength. "Ki-ai" really refers to more than simple shouting; it literally means to "gather (ai) your spirit (ki)." You should focus your entire energy into the winning blow, and one portion of this focus is to shout. This shout should be like a battle-cry, strong and loud enough to penetrate your opponent's heart and pierce his soul. An effective kiai will double the power of your attack.

The use of protective pads is recommended for occasional kumite practice, which will allow the safe delivery of strong attacks and blocks.

To develop further realism and promote your fighting spirit, once you bow to initiate Kumite, never avert your eyes from your opponent until after you have bowed again at the close of Kumite practice. Moreover, keep your eyes on your opponent while bowing. Note that this is distinct from the more relaxed, respectful bow of respect at the start and close of training or among friends and associates.

4. Posture

The form of kamae ("guarding posture") will vary from one instance to another and from person to person depending upon relative size, speed and strength. Be flexible: a single posture is not appropriate for all situations. In all instances, however, the following principles are applicable:

a. Make speedy moves.
b. Stay steady and maintain balance.
c. Don't focus strength in your shoulders.
d. Never "wind up" – that is, do not pull your fist back before punching; punch from where your fist is. Your opponent will anticipate your punch if you first pull back. Instead, learn to maintain your fist at an appropriate distance in basic and combination practice.
e. Similarly, do not draw your hips backward before punching. Your opponent overwhelm you in that split-second.

f. Keep a narrow stance. Drop your hips low. Too wide a stance would prevent you from making an effective forward punch or kick and will slow your movements. Rely on basic practice with low stances to develop strong leg and hip power, which will allow you to assume an effective narrow stance for kumite.

5. Distance

The distance between you and your opponent should be adequate for preventing unexpected attacks from your opponent, yet short enough so that you may reach him. You must practice at varying distances to develop this concept fully. Start with approximately a one-meter distance and adjust with practice.

6. Breathing

Disorder of your mind could lead to disorderly breathing. Train yourself so as to maintain orderly and rhythmic breathing even during violent actions. The principles of breathing as described above are essential.

7. Eyes

It is necessary to practice keeping your eyes still while seeing all. If you move your eyes, your opponent can anticipate your next move. If you focus on your opponent's feet, he can easily strike you with his hands, and vice versa. Direct your vision towards the center of your opponent's chest, around his solar plexus, and focus beyond, rather than on, your opponent. This will help you develop a broader field of vision that can encompass your opponent's hands and feet.

8. Essentials of the Fighting Art (Adapted from Roshi)

Never start a fight. Wait for your opponent's attack.

Stay away from unnecessary trouble. Never jump into a meaningless fight.

If you practice the above two principles, your attack will not appear to be an attack, but rather will seem like a block.

Never underestimate your opponent no matter how weak he may look. The moment you look down on him, you are likely doomed to lose the encounter. Anyone who does not abide by this rule is not qualified to study Karate.

9. Insights into the Fighting Art (Adapted from Sonshi)

a. Combination of orthodox and unorthodox techniques for victory

Simple, orthodox attacks are effective if practiced sufficiently and if delivered with full conviction and proper breathing. Occasionally, however, it may be advantageous to employ unorthodox, irregular attacks.

There are only three primary colors – blue, yellow and red – but by combining these, we generate all of the colors of the rainbow. Similarly, in Karate, we have only two general types of techniques – the orthodox and the unorthodox. But if we combine these, we can generate a spectrum of methods for attacking and blocking.

b. Vulnerability and Invulnerability: Lessons from Water.

You should attack your opponent's vulnerability with your invulnerability. To understand this, consider the behavior of water. Water is not fixed at all. It runs from high to low places. It seeks the simple path and moves around rocks that appear invulnerable. Yet in doing so, it will eventually wear away these invulnerable rocks. Eventually, it can tear down mountains. Like water, avoid invulnerable parts and move your attack towards vulnerable parts. This requires complete flexibility.

CHAPTER 4
Taisabaki

Taisabaki refers to shifting your body speedily left or right to avoid an attack. It is the basis for serious Kumite practice. You may think of your opponent like an arrow coming straight to your center, and you must instantly move to one side. It is often said that an outside block is preferable over an inside block, and that taisabaki is preferable over an outside block. Effective taisabaki can minimize, or even eliminate, the need to block. Recall the lesson from water (above).

1. Hand Attacks

When an attack is made to your face, move the upper part of your body to avoid the attack. Your feet should stay in the same place. You can move your body back or to the side.

Opponent prepares

Lean Back…

…or to the side

When an attack is made to your upper body, bend your knees, drop your waist, and let the attack pass over your head.

2. Leg Attacks

Pull back your waist to avoid a kick. Maintaining balance is essential.

You can avoid a kick by changing the direction of your body.

When trapped in a corner, you can turn your body sideways to slip by the attack. Note that this is a highly advanced technique.

1

2

3

4

5

6

Basic Defense Techniques using Hands and Feet

Nagaishi-Uke (Internal Block)

To block a punch to your upper body, push it inwards (like an outside arm block) with your palm.

Age-Uke with reversed footwork

Block the fist which is attacking your upper body using a rising block, but with the opposite stance. This is the most effective way to block upper punches.

Jodan Juji-Uke

(Upper cross block)

Block the fist that is attacking your upper body by crossing your forearms and blocking with crossed fists. This is especially useful against powerful and speedy attacks. Use a strong stance.

Gedan Juji-Uke (Lower cross block)
Cross your arms at a low position to block a front kick. You can, at the same time, counter-attack your opponent's shin or ankle. Use a strong stance.

Yoko Juji Uke (Side cross block)
This is useful when it is hard to predict where your assailant's attack will strike. Bring one arm in front of your face, like an outside arm block, Place the other arm at a low position, pushing the elbow outwards. A strong counterattack can still be made from this position.

Ryote-Uke (Blocking with both hands)
Bend the elbows of both hands and block your opponent's attacks by twisting your waist. This the most effective method to block powerful kicks.

Sukui-Uke (Scooping block)

When kicked towards your midsection, catch the kick from below in a scooping motion and either hold your opponents foot, or raise it up further, which will knock him down.

Ura-Ken (Backfist)

When attacked by a front kick or side kick, step back half-way and strike the attacking foot with a backfist. This should immobilize your opponent.

Hiza-Uke I (Knee block)

To nullify your opponent's kicks, raise your knee high and block with your shins.

Hiza-Uke II

To cope with continuous attacks by punches or kicks, raise one foot up to protect your lower body, and use your hands to block upper attacks.

CHAPTER 5
Sanbon Kumite (Three-step Sparring)

The importance of Pre-Planned Kumite Practice

This chapter and the subsequent chapter will describe methods to develop fighting skills. Many Karate practitioners, especially the young, wish to begin Jiu Kumite (free sparring) as soon as possible. However, this is a dangerous approach. It must be kept in mind that the goal in Karate, if one must indeed engage in fighting, is to end the encounter with a single block-and-counter combination. To attain this goal, one must devote extensive training to the following pre-planned movements.

If one instead prematurely devotes his or her energies to free sparring, one may indeed develop quick sparring reflexes. However, this individual will not be able to deliver a "killing" decisive blow when the time is ripe, and, as a result, will likely suffer serious injury from a prolonged encounter. Such individuals may also injure each other during practice by failing to develop appropriate control of their attacking techniques. This is not true Karate. The wise student will recognize the following exercises as an essential transition between basic techniques and their application in combat, and will practice them earnestly.

Sanbon Kumite

Attacks and blocking techniques are announced ahead of time by the Instructor, or the offensive side announces where he will attack and with which technique. The offensive side then attacks three times. The defensive side steps back and blocks each attack. Immediately after blocking the third attack, the defensive side executes a strong counter-attack with a Kiai. The defensive side then assumes the offensive role.

You must attack in earnest, using all of your strength without any hesitation or compromise. Your partner knows in advance where you are going to attack, and therefore will be able to safely block or avoid even your fastest techniques. Nevertheless, your opponent must be made to feel that your technique would defeat them if they did not react. In all of the following moves, keep your stances firm and rooted. Offense should execute strong techniques. Defense must apply taisabaki body twisting and shifting whenever possible, rather than just attempting hand blocks.

Some Examples of Upper Attacks and Blocks

1. Rising block vs. Upper punches

Ready Position

Step 1: Offense: Execute a right stepping punch.
Defense: Step back into a front stance and execute a rising block.

Step 2: Offense: Step forward and execute a left stepping punch.
Defense: Step back with your left foot and execute a right rising block.

<u>Step 3</u>: Offense: Step forward and execute a right stepping punch. Defense: Step back with your right foot and execute a left rising block.

<u>Kime</u> With your blocking hand, grab your opponent's punching arm and pull him down to the ground.

Immediately execute a right counter punch to the solar plexus and Ki-ai (shout).

Both sides then resume the final guarding position and bow.

Stay on guard and do not look away from your opponent until your Instructor commands you to do so.

Advanced students may substitute fudo-dachi for front stance.

2. Upper Inside Block vs. Upper punch

Ready position

Step 1:
Offense: Right stepping punch to face.
Defense: Step back with your right leg and upper inside block with your left hand (closed or open).

Step 2:
Offense: Left stepping punch to face.
Defense: Step back with your left leg and upper inside block with your right hand.

Step 3: Offense: Right stepping punch to face. Defense: Step back with your right leg and upper inside block with your left hand.

Kime: Defense right counter punch to midsection and Kiai.

3. Outside arm block vs. Upper punch

Ready position

Step 1: Offense: Right stepping punch to face. Defense: Step back with your right leg and upper outside block with your left hand.

Step 2: Offense: Left stepping punch to face. Defense: Step back with your left leg and upper outside block with your right hand.

Step 3: Offense: Right stepping punch to face. Defense: Step back with your right leg and upper outside block with your left hand.

Kime: Right counter punch to midsection and Kiai.

Some Examples of Midsection Attacks and Blocks

1. Knife-hand block vs. Middle-level punch

Ready position

Step 1: Offense: Right stepping punch to midsection..same techniques can be used for upper-body attack and defense. Defense: Step back with your right leg into a back stance and execute a knife-hand block with your left hand.

Step 2: Offense: Left stepping punch to midsection. Defense: Step back with your left leg into a back stance and execute a knife-hand block with your right hand.

Step 3: Offense: Right stepping punch to midsection.
Defense: Step back with your right leg into a back stance and execute a knife-hand block with your left hand.

Kime: Right counter spearhand to midsection, twisting your hip to add power, and Kiai.

2. Inside Block vs. Middle-level punch

Ready position

Step 1:
Offense: Right stepping punch to midsection.
Defense: Step back with your right leg and inside block with your left hand (closed or open).

Step 2:
Offense: Left stepping punch.
Defense: Step back with your left leg and inside block with your right hand.

Step 3:
Offense: Right stepping punch.
Defense: Step back with your right leg and inside block with your left hand.

Kime: Right counter punch to midsection and Kiai.

3. Down Block vs. Middle punch

Ready position

Step 1: Offense: Right stepping punch to midsection.
Defense: Step back with your right leg and down block with your left hand.

Step 2: Offense: Left stepping punch.
Defense: Step back with your left leg and down block with your right hand.

Step 3: Offense: Right stepping punch.
Defense: Step back with your right leg and down block with your left hand.

Kime: Right counter punch to midsection and Kiai.

Some Examples of Lower (Kicking) Attacks and Blocks

1. Down Block vs. Front Kick

Ready position

Step 1: Offense: Right front kick to midsection. Defense: Step back with your right leg and down block with your left hand.

Step 2: Offense: Left front kick. Defense: Step back with your left leg and down block with your right hand.

Step 3: Offense: Right front kick. Defense: Step back with your right leg and down block with your left hand.

Kime: Right counter punch to midsection or face and Kiai.

2. Scooping Block vs. Front Kick

Ready position

Step 1: Offense: Right front kick to midsection. Defense: Step back with your right leg and execute a scooping block with your left hand.

Step 2: Offense: Left front kick. Defense: Step back with your left leg and execute a scooping block with your right hand.

Step 3: Offense: Right front kick. Defense: Step back with your right leg and execute a scooping block with your left hand. Note that it is easy to upset your opponent's balance.

Kime: Right counter punch to midsection or face and Kiai.

Consider that all of the above were examples. You can easily devise pre-arranged kumite using many additional attacking and blocking combinations.

Gohon-Kumite (Five-attack sparring) for Timing

The applications presented above can also be extended into Gohon Kumite, where the offense delivers the same technique five consecutive times and the defense counters on the fifth time. In Gohon Kumite, the offense can vary the timing and speed of the attacks. This will sharpen the skills of both practitioners.

CHAPTER 6
Ippon Kumite (One-Attack Sparring)

Ippon kumite is divided into Kihon Ippon Kumite and Jiu Ippon Kumite.

Kihon ("basic") Ippon Kumite: In this case, prior arrangements are made to decide the offensive side and the defensive side, as well as the kinds of offensive techniques to be used and the target area. The defensive side maintains a natural stance while the offense assumes a fighting stance. For advanced students, both sides can assume a fighting stance at the outset.

Jiu ("free") Ippon Kumite: In this case, an attack can be made at any time and to any part of the body. Prior arrangements are made as to defensive and offensive sides except for the most advanced students.

Ippon Kumite requires highly sophisticated techniques and powers of perception that can be gained only through untiring practice. Try to discipline yourself until you reach the stage where you can make full attacks accurately and without thinking. Make every effort to get the knack of the advanced techniques. *Since Ippon Kumite is quite dangerous, never relax your mind.*

Some Examples of Hand Techniques

1. Offense: Upper stepping punch.
Defense: Open-hand outside block and reverse punch

Kamae (ready positions):
Offense takes a left downblock and Defense assumes a natural stance, or, as shown, both sides assume a sparring stance.

Uke (the attack):
Offense executes a right stepping punch to the face. Defense slides left foot towards the outside of the offense's punching arm, and executes an open-hand outside block.

Kime (finishing blow):
Defense executes a right reverse punch to the midsection

Offense: Upper stepping punch
Defense: Forward punch

Kamae (ready positions): Offense takes a left downblock, Defense assumes a natural stance.

Uke (the attack): Offense executes a right stepping punch to the face. Defense slides forward and sideways, outside of the offense's punching arm, and turns his body halfway to avoid the punch

Kime (finishing blow): Defense executes a right reverse punch to the midsection.

3. Offense: Upper stepping punch
Defense: Iron hammer block and backfist

Kamae (ready positions): Offense takes a left downblock, Defense assumes a natural stance.

Uke (the attack): Offense executes a right stepping punch to the face. Defense steps back and executes an outside arm block.

Kime (finishing blow): After blocking, defense executes a right back fist to the face.

4. Offense: midsection stepping punch
Defense: elbow block and backfist

Kamae (ready positions): Offense takes a left downblock, Defense assumes a natural stance.

Uke (the attack): Offense executes a right stepping punch to the midsection. Defense steps back into a horse stance and executes an outside elbow block.

Kime (finishing blow): After blocking, defense executes a back fist to the face.

5. Offense: Upper stepping punch

Defense: Inside block and knife-hand strike

<u>Kamae</u> (ready positions): Offense takes a left downblock, Defense assumes a natural stance.

<u>Uke</u> (the attack): Offense executes a right stepping punch to the face. Defense pivots in place towards the right and executes an inside arm block.

<u>Kime</u> (finishing blow): After blocking, defense turns his body back towards the opponent and executes a knife-hand strike to the neck.

6. Offense: Midsection stepping punch
Defense: Parry block with side-step and knife-hand strike

Kamae (ready positions): Offense takes a right downblock, Defense assumes a guarded knife stance. (Natural or sparring stance could also be used)

Uke (the attack): Offense executes a left stepping punch to the midsection.

Defense parries the punch with a left open-hand outside arm block while moving his left foot forward and twisting to the left to avoid the punch.

Kime (finishing blow): After blocking, defense turns his body around forcefully and executes a knife-hand strike to the neck.

7. Offense: Midsection stepping punch
Defense: Backfist to punch and palm-heel strike

Kamae (ready positions):

Uke (the attack): Offense executes a right stepping punch to the midsection.

Defense steps back at an angle towards the outside of the punch and executes a backfist onto the punching hand or elbow (depending upon distance)

Kime (finishing blow): With the same hand, defense executes a palm-heel strike to the jaw.

8. Offense: Midsection stepping punch
Defense: Revolving block and spear-hand strike

Uke (the attack): Offense executes a right stepping punch to the midsection. Defense remains in natural stance and catches the punch with a cross-hands block.

Defense turns his body to the right while swinging the block up and across his body to the right. Defense continues to parry the punch in a long circular motion to the lower left with the left hand while withdrawing the right hand for a punch.

Kime (finishing blow): Defense executes a right reverse punch twisting the right hip sharply forward.

Some Examples of Leg Techniques

1. Offense: Front kick. Defense: Downblock and reverse punch

Kamae
(ready position)

Uke (the attack): Offense executes a right front kick to the midsection.

Defense steps back and executes a left downblock as he turns his body to the right. Defense parries the punch in a long circular motion to the lower left with the left hand, while withdrawing the right hand for a punch.

Kime (finishing blow): Defense shifts towards the opponent and executes a right reverse punch.

2. Offense: Front kick. Defense: Scooping block & reverse punch

Kamae (ready positions): Offense takes a left downblock, Defense assumes a natural stance.

Uke (the attack): Offense executes a right front kick to the midsection. Defense shifts and turns his body to the right, outside of the kick, and scoops it with his left hand. Defense continues to parry the punch in a long circular motion to the lower left with the left hand, while withdrawing the right hand for a punch.

Kime (finishing blow): Defense executes a right reverse punch.

3. Offense: Front roundhouse kick
Defense: Knife-hand block & reverse punch

Kamae (ready positions):

Uke (the attack): Offense executes a right front roundhouse kick to the midsection. Defense lowers his body and blocks with a left knife-hand.

Kime (finishing blow): Defense shifts towards the offensive and executes a right reverse punch.

4. Offense: Back kick
Defense: Outside block and reverse punch

Kamae (ready positions):

Uke (the attack): Offense turns and executes a right back kick. Defense shifts his body to the left and executes an outside block.

Kime (finishing blow): Defense executes a right reverse punch.

5. Offense: Front kick. Defense: Knee-up block and reverse punch

Kamae (ready positions):

Uke (the attack): Offense executes a right front kick to the midsection. Defense raises the left knee to block.

Defense jabs (Front hand).

Kime (finishing blow): Defense lowers his waist and executes a right reverse punch.

6. Offense: Back round kick. Defense: Duck and stepping punch

Kamae (ready positions):

Uke (the attack): Offense spins around and executes a right back roundhouse kick to the head. Defense ducks low under the kick, remaining on guard.

Kime (finishing blow): Defense quickly rises as the kick passes and executes a right stepping punch.

7. Offense: Upper stepping punch
Defense: Shift and flying front (double) kick

Kamae (ready positions):

Uke (the attack): Offense executes a right stepping punch to the head. Defense shifts his front foot slightly forward and to the left twists his body to the right to avoid the punch and kicks the midsection.

Kime (finishing blow): Without putting the kicking leg down defense quickly executes a left front kick.

8. Offense: Midsection or upper stepping punch
Defense: Shift and front roundhouse kick

Kamae (ready positions):

Uke (the attack): Offense spins around and executes a right back roundhouse kick to the head. Defense twists his body to the right to avoid the punch

Kime (finishing blow): Defense executes a right front roundhouse kick to the head.

9. Offense: Step-up jab. Defense: Flying side kick

Kamae (ready positions): Offense takes a sparring stance downblock, Defense assumes a natural stance (as shown) or sparring stance.

Uke (the attack): Offense brings the rear leg up, then jabs as he brings the front leg forward into a sparring stance. Defense shifts back and to the right to avoid the jab.

Kime (finishing blow): Defense executes a right flying side kick to the head or midsection.

CHAPTER 7
Throwing Techniques

Karate also incorporates throwing techniques. However, they are similar to blocking or tai-sabaki in that they are not an end unto themselves. Throwing techniques in Karate are all characterized by the application of a finishing blow and perhaps a joint lock.

Palm Attack and Throwing

In order to throw and Opponent who is driving forward with a technique such as a Stepping Punch, it is very important to situate yourself with flexibility according to his movements. In general, try to position yourself on the inside of his line of attack.

Ready positions

Block his attack with a Knife Hand

Pull his arm using your blocking hand, and Palm Heel Strike his chin while sweeping his leg.

Maintain a grip on his arm while you complete the throw so he cannot roll away. Deliver Finishing Blow.

Punch to the Knee Followed by a Throw

Ready positions

As your Opponent launches his attack, drop down to avoid it.

Punch your Opponent's knee

Scoop your Opponent's heel

Lift his leg, throwing him to the ground

Finishing blow

Catching a Punch and Throwing

Ready positions

Catch your Opponent's punch with both hands

Pull your Opponent closer and sweep his leg

Throw him to
the ground

Finishing
blow

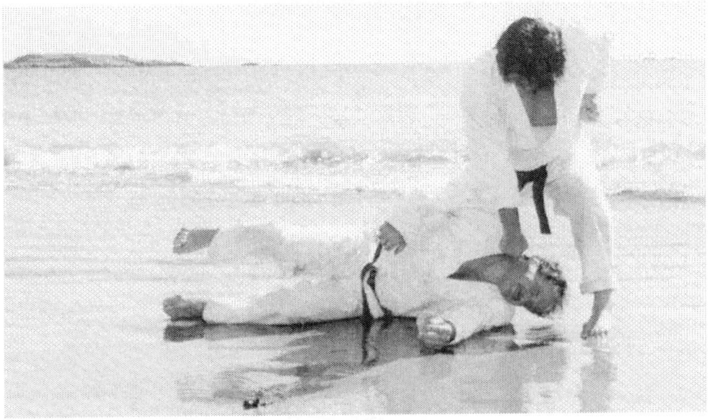

Encircling the Neck and Throwing

Ready positions

Move to the outside of your Opponent. As you block his punch wrap your arms around his neck.

Pull your Opponent's down

Finishing blow

Collaring the Opponent and Throwing

Ready positions

As your Opponent approaches, move in and grab his collar.

Maintain a grip on his collar, pull him forward and sweep his leg from the outside

Finishing blow

Throwing Techniques against Kicks Most people think it is difficult to block a kick, let alone follow through with a throw. The truth is that the opponent is imbalanced when kicking. Unlike a punch, where he is standing on both legs, a kick forces him to rely on one leg for support, and makes his balance less stable. This provides an opportunity for a throw.

Scooping a Front Kick and Throwing

Ready positions

As your Opponent kicks, move to the outside and scoop his kicking leg

Lift and lock his leg.

Continue to lift and throw him.

Finishing blow

Twisting a Front Kick and Throwing

Ready positions

Receive his Front Kick with a scoop.

Move in and execute a Palm Strike to his knee

Twist his leg to throw him

Finishing blow

Scooping a Side Kick and Throwing

Ready positions

Move to the inside and scoop his side kick

As you hold and lock his leg, move in and grab his collar

Sweep his rear leg

Finishing blow

CHAPTER 8
Fifteen Forms of Ko-Bo

The KoBo are combinations designed to help acquire proper timing, speed, power and stance. Once they become familiar, they should be performed in continuous motion, without hesitation between techniques.

KoBo Shodan KoBo Shodan is centered around the Horse-Riding Stance and Elbow techniques. The intent behind using this stance is to maintain a balanced state. Practice repeatedly to build a stance full of vitality and power.

1.Horse-Riding Stance and Double-Hand Block Form

Ready positions

Offense attacks with a stepping punch. Defense steps in with a kibadachi and executes an upper arm double-block.

Without hesitation, defense executes a backfist to the face.

Defense shifts rear foot towards opponent, simultaneous-ly grabbing his punch (rear hand) and striking the neck with a front knifehand

In a continuous motion, defense pushes the shoulder over, while pulling the rear hand, stepping over with his front leg and sweeping the opponent.

Finishing the throw, defense executes a counter punch. Note: maintain grip on the opponent's punching arm to prevent him rolling away.

A joint lock could be applied after the punch.

2. Horse-Riding Stance and Elbow-Attack Form

Ready positions

Offense attacks with a stepping punch. Defense steps in and blocks the opponent's punch with a knife hand block

Completed knife hand block shown from opposite side for clarity.

Defense continues to step forward into a kibadachi, grabbing his punch (rear hand) and executes an elbow stike to the face.

Defense ducks and executes an elbow strike to the ribs, maintaining control of the opponent's hand.

Defense rises, and executes a shuto to the neck.

The remaining moves are similar to form number 1.

(shown from opposite side for clarity)

Continue the sweep while pulling his arm and pushing his shoulder/neck.

After completing the throw, Defense executes a finishing punch.

3. Horse-Riding Stance and Scissors-Block Form

Ready positions

Offense attacks with a stepping punch. Defense steps outside of the attack into a kibadachi and executes an upper arm double-block, left arm outside and right arm inside the attacking arm.

Defense slips behind the opponent by bringing the rear leg around into a front stance, simultaneously twising his double-arm block, pulling the opponent's arm while pushing the opponent's shoulder down.

Maintaining controls of the opponent's arms, Defense brings his rear leg up, and steps over the opponents leg…

… and sweeps the opponent's leg while pushing down on his shoulder.

During the throw, Defense pulls the opponent's arm over his own knee, and now breaks the elbow with a palm heel strike.

Keeping control of the opponent, Defense steps towards the front.

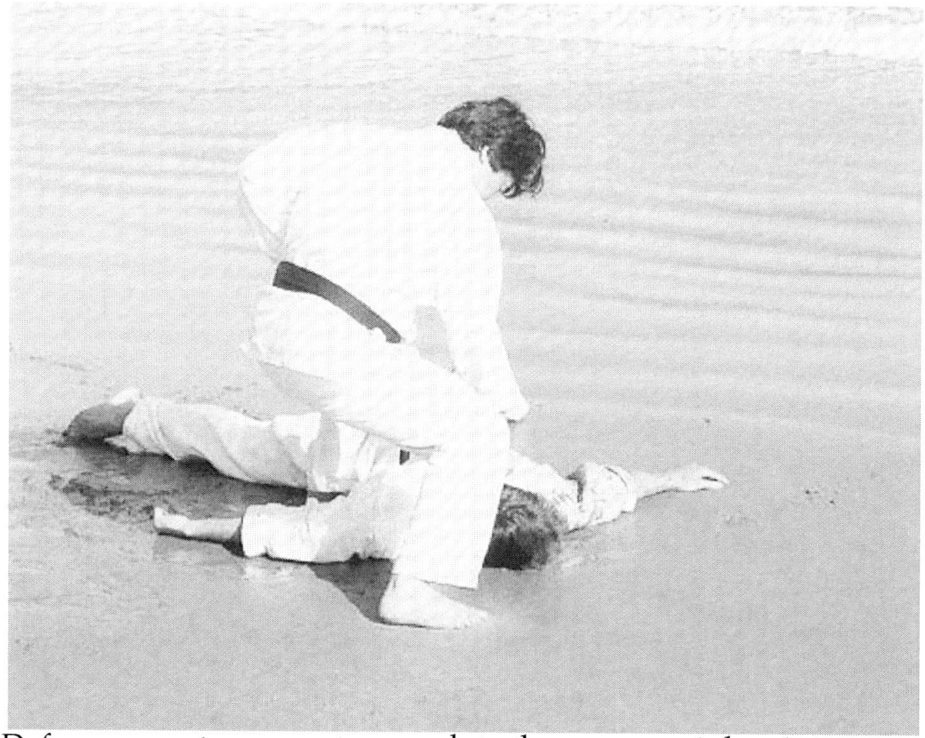

Defense executes a counter punch to the opponent's head. A joint lock could be applied after the punch.

4. Horse-Riding Stance and Back Elbow-Attack Form

Kamae (ready positions)

Offense attacks with a stepping punch. Defense steps in with a kibadachi and elbow strikes the Opponent's ribs.

Defense chambers his right fist into his open left hand.

Defense spins in the opposite direction and executes an elbow strike to the head.

Defense pushes the shoulder over, while pulling the rear hand, stepping over with his front leg and sweeps the opponent.

Finishing the throw, defense executes a counter punch. Note: maintain grip on the opponent's punching arm to prevent him rolling away.

A joint lock could be applied after the punch.

5. Horse-Riding Stance and Spinning Elbow-Attack Form

Kamae (ready positions)

Offense attacks with a stepping punch. Defense steps into the attack.

Defense parries the punch with an open-hand block as he moves to the outside.

Defense spins around into a KibaDachi and delivers an elbow strike to the Opponent's ribs.

In a continuous motion from the above movement, defense continues to spin and grabs the Opponent's shoulders or head from behind.

Maintainin
g a grip on
the
Opponent,
Defense
continues
his spin
into a Front
Stance.

Defense executes a knee strike as he pulls the Opponent down. He then delivers a Finishing Blow

A joint lock could be applied after the punch.

KoBo Nidan

This KoBo consists mainly of kicks, including the Hook Kick, Back Kick, Back Roundhouse Kick, Double Kick and Scissors Kick. By practicing very hard, the breadth of your attacks should increase. Most of these involve a half-spin, which should be executed as a smooth movement.

1. Back Kick Form

Ready positions

Block Opponent's punch with a Crescent Kick

Turn counter clockwise and prepare for a Back Kick

Back Kick to MidSection

Bring your foot down

Continue with a Stepping Punch to Opponent's face

2. Hook Kick Form

Ready positions

Execute a Crescent Kick to Block your Opponent's Punch

Get Ready to Return your kicking leg.

Hook kick your Opponent's face.

Bring your kicking leg to the Rear.

Launch a Round Kick to the Opponent' s Face

Place the kicking leg forward

Continue forward with a Stepping Punch to the Face

3. Spin Form
Ready positions

Execute a Crescent Kick to Block your Opponent's Punch

Continue turning in the same direction and prepare for a Back Roundhous e Kick

Continue spinning and execute a Back Roundhous e Kick to Opponent's Head

Place your kicking leg to the front

Launch a Round Kick to the Opponent's Face. Execute these kicks in a continuous, spinning motion. Add a stepping punch if he has not fallen.

4. Double Jump Kick Form

Ready positions

Shift back diagonally to avoid your Oppon-ent's Punch and block with a Knife Hand

Front Kick to the Opponent's ribs

Execute a Jumping Double Kick

5. Flying Side Kick Form

Jump to the side to avoid your Opponent's Attack

Continue the jumping motion and chamber your leg

Execute a Flying Side Kick (Shown from opposite angle for clarity)

KoBo Sandan

Diverse techniques are included in this KoBo, such as the Spinning Knife Hand, and Pendulum Attack. Practicing these techniques will enable you to move your body smoothly, and the offense and defense techniques will become fluid.

Spinning Knife-Hand Form

Ready position

Block your Opponent's punch from the outside

Continue turning clockwise

Execute a Spinning Knife-Hand to his neck.

Back Fist Form
Ready position

Duck to dodge your Opponent's punch, and counter punch to his midsection

Swing your arm back

Execute a Pendulum strike with a Back Fist to his groin

Lower your body and hook your arm under his front leg

Scoop his leg

Finishing blow

Arm Form

Ready position

Dodge your Opponent's punch by stepping backwards

Scoop his punching arm

Turn your body and twist his arm

Stepping in under his arm, punch his elbow

Continue to turn, twisting his arm

Pull him down

Finishing blow

Sword Hand Form

Ready position

Block his punch with a Knife Hand

Grab his punching arm and Knife Hand Strike to his neck

Step around forcefully, pulling his arm and pushing his neck

Continue to twist your body and pull him down

Continue to turn, twisting his arm

Finishing blow

Defense against a Knife Hand

Ready position

Shift your body forward and block your Opponent's overhead Knife Hand Strike with a Rising Block

Grab his attacking arm

Step in with your back leg and twist his arm

Pull your Opponent down

Finishing blow

VOLUME IV:
Basic Philosophy

CHAPTER 1
Breathing and Heart

Introduction: Three Types of Ki

For the Karate practitioner, correct breathing is essential. Breathing plays the leading role in life processes and affects the health of the body and spirit. Proper breathing improves blood circulation, regulates heartbeat, and strengthens internal organs. It promotes good heath, willpower, resistance to disease, and brings forth spiritual strength that is "life power".

Let us consider briefly how breathing can alter this life power, which is classically referred to as "Ki." Traditionally, there are three types of breathing in relationship to Ki: natural, nourished and violent. Natural Ki refers to the fetus' breath within the mother's womb. This is a passive sort of breathing. Once born, however, the individual becomes active and must make life choices. The good person is calm and maintains a broad outlook on life. This person seeks perfection and nourishes his or her Ki using some of the breathing techniques described herein. In contrast, a bad person angers easily and is narrow-minded. He or she develops an un-nourished, violent Ki.

Proper development of Ki awakens a strong spirit. Without development, your true self remains asleep. Ki is to spirit as mother is to child. Nourish your Ki and give rise to your own unfolding spirit.

Breathing and the Heart

The heart is controlled by the autonomic nervous system. This system consists of two opposing forces - the sympathetic nervous system and the parasympathetic nervous system. One result of these two opposing forces is the regulation of heart activity.

Over-tension, excitement, anxiety, surprise and fright increase the heart's burden. Physical or mental discomfort results when these two systems are unbalanced.

Proper breathing restores the correct balance and peace of mind. Correct breathing correlates with composure gained through meditation. Exhale slowly to relieve tension. Worry and stress increase the heart's burden, but laughter comforts the heart. Remember to laugh.

Penetrating pain in the heart during the early stages of running indicates that the bloodstream has insufficient oxygen. As an example of the power of proper breathing on the heart, flex your stomach muscles and exhale deeply while running, which will allow your heart to enrich itself and increase bloodstream oxygen. Proper breathing will allow your heart to sustain emotional as well as physical burdens.

In the following sections, we will discuss further how to breathe most effectively.

Tanden Breathing versus Chest Breathing

In Western societies, individuals often develop "chest-centered" breathing, rather than the Tanden (abdomen-centered) breathing common of Eastern tradition. Despite good intentions and effort, chest breathing is really very shallow, and does not allow exchange of much of the air within one's lungs. It decreases the efficiency of the body and results in loss of appetite and vigor. Tanden breathing, however, results in better health and improves your general outlook on life. To do this, relax your shoulders and chest, and breathe in and out by expanding and contracting your abdominal muscles. This will pull and push your diaphragm, which will promote maximal air exchange with each breath. This is the opposite of the "stomach in, chest out" command often heard in Western schools and military organizations. Begin exhaling as much as possible, after which you will naturally inhale deeply. Deep exhalations maximize air exchange and release unknown powers in the body. Even if an inhalation is short, always exhale as strongly as possible. You may exhale through your mouth or nose, but always inhale through your nose. This is essential since the passage-ways of your nose both filter and warm the air before it reaches your lungs. Air that is inhaled through your mouth reaches your lungs cold (which inhibits oxygen uptake) and unfiltered (which deposits impurities in your lungs and damages them). During heavy exercise, the tendency may be to "pant" through your mouth. However, deep tanden breathing from the start will avoid this situation and maintain your vitality during training.

People who practice tanden breathing, even if normally short of breath or suffering from chest pain, are able to carry out lengthy and seemingly impossible tasks without tiring.

Tanden Breathing and Power

Proper breathing aids the spiritless and vain, the show-off and the hysteric. People with inferior self-images are also helped by tanden breathing. They can become forthright, perceptive and confident. The stubborn, picky or narrow-minded have a "stiffness" in their stomach that can be remedied by tanden breathing.

Maintain constant flexing of the abdominal muscles whether inhaling or exhaling. Contract only abdominal muscles while relaxing others, especially those of the throat and chest. Those who wish to master the martial arts must master this first.

Breathe with your abdomen every day and your body movements will become lighter and fluid. You will attain mental stability and be able to tolerate change. You will also be able to maintain your center and confront an opponent calmly. With continued practice of tanden breathing, willpower is strengthened and a more mature and positive outlook on life is acquired.

Vitality and Tanden Breathing

People who use their heads more than their bodies easily become neurotic. Tanden breathing can help reverse this trend. Sit straight, otherwise your breathing will be restricted to chest breathing. Maintain tanden breathing during mental tasks and you will promote vitality and accomplish more.

Anger Disrupts Breathing

Anger disturbs natural breathing by causing your chest to tighten. The resulting pressure in your chest also causes increased pressure on your brain, restricts your heart and, over time, will shorten your life expectancy.

Breathing for Offensive and Defensive Methods in Karate

In Karate practice, inhale on defensive moves and exhale on offensive moves. Focus your concentration in your abdomen. Tighten your sphincter muscle while inhaling and relax it while exhaling. You should inhale quietly, gradually and continuously through your nose, so that your opponent cannot detect your breathing pattern. If not executing an offensive move, you should exhale nasally in time with your opponent's movements. When executing an offensive technique, exhale forcefully through your mouth. Do this also should your breathing become interrupted, so that you can regain your proper harmony. Remain calm throughout an encounter.

Breathing and Saliva

Parotine is a hormone found in saliva that promotes youthfulness and hinders aging. Saliva, when swallowed, eventually reaches your kidneys and maintains vigor. During Karate practice, place your tongue lightly on the upper part of your mouth, behind your front teeth. This will encourage the flow of saliva.

The Appropriate time to Practice Breathing

Practice breathing after a bath or shower. At this time your body and mind will be refreshed, circulation will be good and your muscles will be relaxed. Find a peaceful place to sit with clean air. The best hours for this are between midnight and noon.

Breathe with Nature

When you practice breathing during a quiet time, try to let yourself feel that you are part of the natural order. First, exhale deeply several times, which will put your mind at ease. When you inhale, concentrate on filling your body with the spirit of the universe. Then exhale slowly and quietly. You are not only part of nature, but nature is also part of you. Once you feel part of nature, your life will be healthier.

"Zen"

CHAPTER 2
Practical Exercises in Breathing and Meditation

In this chapter, we will present various exercises, building upon tanden breathing, that will provide revitalizing energy after physical training, studying/mental tasks, and everyday life.

Zazen and Breathing

Zazen is both physical and mental. The two sitting positions for Zazen are referred to as the "full lotus position" and the "half lotus position." The full lotus requires placing the left foot on the right thigh, and the right foot on the left thigh. This requires practice. The half lotus, in which only one foot is on the thigh of the opposite leg, is appropriate for beginners or those who are not very flexible. For either position, sit on a flat pillow or mat, about 7cm in height. Both knees should touch the floor. Position your upper body such that your nose and navel form a straight line perpendicular to the floor. Rest your hands at your lower abdomen, relax your shoulders, straighten your back, and focus your vision approximately 1 meter to the front.

Exhale deeply to rid your lungs of old air. Open your lips very slightly, and exhale slowly over a long period of time. Repeat this several times. Then close your mouth and breathe only through your nose. Let your tongue lightly touch the back of your upper teeth. Let your breathing remain quiet, subtle and continuous. Should a cramp develop, open your lips and slowly exhale.

Kinhinho

Kinhinho is "walking Zen" and is especially helpful when tired, dull or sleepy after long hours of study or work. It refreshes and restores sharpness and clear thinking.

Stand and put both hands over the lower part of your lungs. Stretch your back and place your line of vision about 2 meters in front of you. As with seated "Zazen," purify your lungs five or six times. Then, put one foot in front of you and slowly exhale as you place it on the floor. Next, put the other foot in front and slowly inhale. Flex your abdomen during inhalation. Breathe in time with your steps. Feel as if you are breathing to your lower abdomen. Stretch your legs until they are perfectly straight and concentrate carefully on each step. Walk at a rate of about one meter per minute. After six cycles you will naturally change from chest breathing to tanden breathing. Continue with this exercise for about 15 minutes, and you will be ready to continue studying or working.

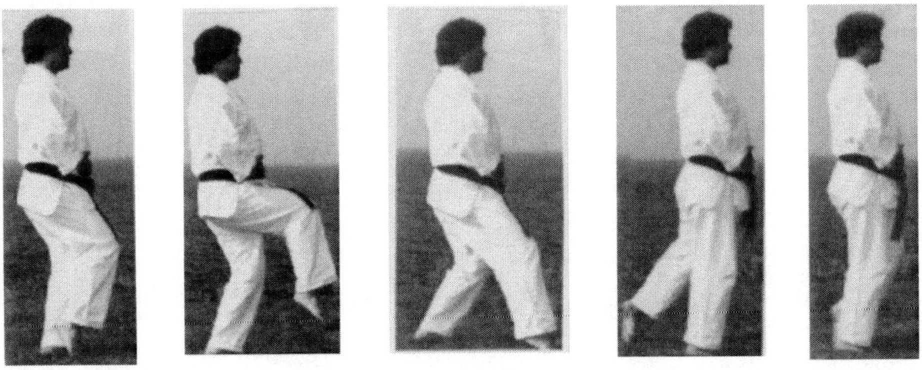

Nai Kan Ho

This method is a collection of breathing exercises useful for relaxing your spirit and body. It will promote health if practiced morning and night. In addition, it provides tremendous revitalization if practiced at the close of a Karate training session. Even after the most arduous training, Nai Kan Ho will refresh you.

1. Lie down on your back and stretch out, legs naturally apart and arms naturally extended slightly from your sides.
2. Close your eyes. It is acceptable to narrow your eyes and look straight upward. Should perspiration enter and sting your eyes, blink to wash it away.
3. Press your tongue lightly behind your teeth and close your mouth lightly.

4. Breathe in slowly through your nose.
5. Swallow your saliva and pull your breath to your lower abdomen.
6. Exhale through your mouth and relax your abdomen.
7. Repeat this 3 to 4 times.
8. Next, pull your breath to your knees, and as you exhale, relax your knees.
9. Repeat this 3 to 4 times.
10. Next, pull your breath to your toes, and as you exhale, relax your toes.
11. Repeat this 3 or 4 times.
12. Finally, pull your breath throughout your whole body, and as your exhale, relax your entire body.
13. Repeat this 3 or 4 times.
14. Breathe only through your nose a few times, open your eyes and focus upward on one spot.
15. Slowly sit up. Compose your spirit as in Zazen.
16. Slowly stand up. Take your time.
17. Relax your neck
18. Raise your arms above your head and stretch up on your toes.
19. Feel as if you are releasing energy from your arms, then lower them.
20. Take a slow deep breath.

This technique will cause your fatigue from training to vanish, and you will feel much better.

Gyogazen

Gyogazen is a form of meditation that should be practiced for 30 minutes first thing in the morning and just before sleep.

Close your eyes and empty your mind of all thought. Stretch your body. Repeat to yourself, "My body is relaxed, my nerves are relaxed." Lie flat and straighten both legs, heels together. Your nose, navel and feet should be in one line. Relax your mouth and lightly touch your tongue to the back of your upper teeth. Rest both hands on your abdomen. Flex your abdomen while you inhale deeply through your nose. Inhale for a few seconds and exhale twice as long. Keep your mouth closed throughout.

Stretch both arms in the air and bring your hands together. Stare at them, concentrating on opening them. Slowly open your hands and allow them to drift about 30 centimeters apart. Command them to stop, and order them to come together. Repeat this exercise several times, and you will fall into a deep trance- like state.

During the time in which you are moving your hands, make suggestions to yourself. What you suggest depends upon your immediate purposes and circumstances. Consider your specific goal(s) for the day, and repeat to yourself, "All is going well; I can succeed at my task."

At the close of morning gyogazen practice, tell yourself, "This will be a good day. I can accomplish my goals." Then get up, maintain your positive attitude and do so. After evening gyogazen practice, tell yourself, "The day is over. I forgive myself and others, and shall sleep well." With your mind in order, fall asleep. In this manner, you can use gyogazen to organize your day.

Methods of Inhaling and Exhaling

This breathing exercise promotes confidence to withstand an opponent and to complete any task. This method of will incorporate the "Hangetsu", or "half-moon" Karate stance. Stand loosely with your feet pointing slightly inward. Lower your hips and sink into your knees, allowing them to bow naturally. Inhale deeply through your nose. Tighten your sphincter muscle and contract your stomach. Elevate the area under your armpits and tighten your chest. Flex your sides, and form fists.

Slowly and strongly exhale, contracting your body, and make a hissing sound through your mouth. Do not relax. Keep your muscles and your Ki tight and focused. Repeat this exercise until you feel that you have reached your maximum degree of "body-mind tension." Sustain that state. You should feel immovable. With your Ki flexed, your mind and body unify. Even if someone hit you, you would not feel it.

General Stretching and Breathing

For all exercises, including "warm-ups" and calisthenics, exhale while bending, and inhale while straightening. This will increase your stretching ability, prevent strain and fatigue during exercise, and promote your general health.

Chapter 3

Twenty Golden Lessons of Master Funakoshi

Careful attention to these lessons will help the student attain a much deeper understanding of Karate.

1. "In Karate, start with a bow and finish with a bow"
   Do not forget the spirit of the bow in daily life as well.

2. "There is no first attack in Karate".
   Never start a fight with fists or with words.

3. "Karate is a great assistance to justice"
   Challenge injustice in your community and in the world.

4. "Know yourself at first and then others"
   It is extremely difficult to know oneself, but nonetheless, you must examine yourself as often as you can, and at the same time judge others intelligently.

5. "Spirit first, techniques second"
   The right spirit helps develop good techniques.

6. "Be ready to release your mind"
   Keep a free, relaxed mind.

7. "Accidents come out of idleness"
   Be cautious even in relaxation.

8. "Do not think that you can learn Karate only in the Dojo"
   Apply Karate to your daily life. Never forget the spirit of respect for people.

9. "It will take your entire life to learn Karate"
   Practice as long as you live. You will be continually improving spirit as well as techniques.

10. "Karate-ize everything"
    Apply the spirit of Karate to everything in life, and you will develop a deeper Karate.

11. "Karate is just like hot water. If you do not give heat constantly, it will again become cold water"
    Unless you keep training, your technique will deteriorate.

12. "Do not think that you have to win. Think, rather that you do not have to lose"

If you focus on winning, you will be tense and therefore will be less effective. If, however, you have confidence that you will not lose, you can remain relaxed and flexible, and in this condition have a much better chance of winning.

13. "Victory depends upon your ability to tell vulnerable points from invulnerable ones"

Attack only vulnerable targets. Always appreciate that in even one second your opponent might sway from a position of strength to one of vulnerability.

14. "Move according to your opponent"

Be flexible and have good Karate eyes.

15. "Consider your opponent's hands and legs to be sharp swords"

Make a habit of suspecting that your opponent has a sharper and faster sword than you, so that you will always be cautious.

16. "As soon as you leave home for work, think that millions of opponents are waiting for you"

Be ready at all times.

17. "Low stance for beginners, high stance for advanced students"

Take as low a stance as possible in order to build up muscles and to stabilize your stance. After achieving black belt, you can take as high a stance as you like if you can demonstrate that your high stance is effective.

18. "Practicing kata is one thing, engaging in a real fight is another"

Perform a kata correctly and be loyal to basic techniques. In a fight, however, you must be flexible and adapt to your opponent's position, distance, ground, etc.

19. "Do not forget (1) strength and weakness of power, (2) bending down and stretching up of body, and (3) slowness and speed of techniques.

These refer to power, speed and timing. Be flexible and do not use energy unnecessarily.

20. "Devise at all times"

If you punch 20 times, each of these punches is quite different. Repeat your techniques until you can perform them as you want to. Unless you advance every day, you are doomed to retreat.

CHAPTER 4
Golden Lessons from Master Obata

Gichin Funakoshi was responsible for bringing Karate to Japan. Continued spread of Karate throughout Japan, and eventually the world, relied on the efforts of subsequent generations of Karate Masters. Master Isao Obata, the oldest and first student of Master Funakoshi, and teacher of the author of this book, is one of these Masters. Professor Obata preferred to remain in the background, and as such, he is not as widely known as some of his contemporaries. Here we present, for the first time, selected writings of Master Obata.

1. **Bow.** Always bow in respect and with an expansive heart. In this way, harmony is expressed and maintained. Be steadfast in working towards elevating your spirit towards this goal.

2. **Realize that refining and cultivating one's spirit to reach enlightenment is the true meaning of life.** It is only through sweat and devotion to spiritual and mental training that enlightenment is attained.

3. **Do not be impatient** Strive towards your goal with slow, steady steps.

4. **Study and try, think and try, ask questions and try, invent ways to attain realizations. Repeat these steps over and over.** Repetition is the best, and the shortest, way to attain true understanding.

5. **The basic conditions necessary for advancement in Karate** Assume a strong, unwavering stance. Breathe from your abdomen, to absorb the vast spiritual energy of the universe. This will open your mind's eye, and you will be able to use this gift for the betterment of mankind.

6. **Training** Pain and adversity are intrinsic to training. An explosive start is vital to train each part of your body to become a weapon. This explosive force derives from your stance. Make pursuit of this goal a priority.

7. Man's spirit is weak To overcome one's natural spiritual weakness, you must have a positive, natural attitude and be aware of your limitations.

8. Maintain the dignity, expansive nature and gracious aura of heart which you attain through the study of Karate Strive to comprehend the meaning of "Purity in nothingness." This is where true enlightenment will be found. It will allow you to live your life without resentments or regrets.

9. The sun rises in the sky Strive to bring the universe, the physical world and your inner spiritual world into sharp focus. The truth arising from this focus will provide spiritual "food" that will nourish you as you strive towards enlightenment.

Strive to master these principles of the purity of Karate.

CHAPTER 5
Some Thoughts from the Masters

Essentials of the Fighting Art by Roshi

Never start a fight. Wait for your opponent to attack.

Stay away from unnecessary trouble. Never jump into a meaningless fight.

Never under-rate your opponent no matter how weak he may look. The moment you look down on him, you are doomed to death. Anyone who does not abide by this rule is not qualified to learn Karate.

Three kinds of Swords

Tenshi no Ken: the Sword of God controls barbarians and keeps the four seasons, nature and the human world in order. It generates negative and positive power that sustains the life of the universe. It activates growth in the spring and summer, and ends it with the freezing of fall and winter. This sword can tear up clouds in the sky and cut the ground in half. Once this sword is raised, every king on earth sets himself in order and prepares to listen.

Shoko no Ken: the Sword of Kings is made of intelligence, bravery, integrity, sagacity, loyalty and fortitude. It never loses. The sword follows the rule of heaven, for it abides by the movements of the sun, the moon and the stars. It follows the rule of the earth, for it abides by the changes of the four seasons. It calms the minds of people and the seven seas. This is the sword of friendship, peace and the growth of nations.

Shonin no Ken: the Sword of the Unenlightened always looks for meaningless trouble. It cuts through necks and arms, and cuts the heart out. It has no control over itself. Once it loses the fight, it is totally lost. Not only is it no help to nations, it is also harmful to them.

Which sword would you like to develop by studying karate?

Fighting Art by Sonshi

The combination of orthodox and unorthodox techniques

Use mainly orthodox techniques, but occasionally, if it is to your advantage, employ an irregular technique. There are only 5 basic colors – blue, red, yellow, black and white – but when we combine these, we have an infinite number of colors. In Karate, combining the two basic types of techniques – orthodox and unorthodox – allows us to generate an almost infinite number of ways to attack and defend.

Vulnerability and Invulnerability

Attack your opponent's vulnerability with your invulnerability. You can triumph by turning your opponent's strength, desire and confidence into invulnerability.

Charge freely

Examine your opponent's and your situation to determine who has the advantage.

Provoke him a little to see if he responds quickly.

Put your opponent into a fixed situation in order to determine his most vulnerable point.

Start a small fight to see his exact intention, strength and weakness.

Be like water

Water is not fixed at all. It runs from high to low places. In fighting, invulnerable parts should be avoided and weaker parts attacked. This requires complete flexibility.

Three lessons by Goshi

Make a serious effort to understand others if you wish to succeed at very difficult tasks.

Abide by principles at all times.

Attend always to the principle of "Do." Work with an empty and open mind, and always remember the spirit of duty and honesty, the spirit of the bow, and the spirit of mutual cooperation, trust and compassion.

Unless a nation abides by these principles, it will eventually perish.

CHAPTER 6
The Secret Meaning of "Kara-Te"

Mastery of Karate involves much more than techniques. The term Karate-Do is often used to describe life-long practice and incorporation of principles of Karate to one's entire life. There is yet a deeper level of understanding of Karate-Do.

Some time after Master Funakoshi Gichin brought Karate from Okinawa to Japan, he recognized that the art had developed considerably from the original Chinese art of "Te." Until this time the word "Kara-Te" actually referred to "Chinese (Kara) Hand (Te)." Funakoshi took the bold step of replacing "Kara" referring to "Chinese" with the identical-sounding Japanese word "Kara" meaning "empty". The written characters for these two words differ, despite that they sound the same. If this is confusing, consider the English words "hear" and "here", which sound the same, yet are written differently and have different meanings. Funakoshi made this change to denote the further development of the art in Japan, and to establish it as a true Japanese art.

Karate as set forth by Funakoshi referred to "Empty (Kara) Hand (Te)." The simplest level of interpretation refers to an empty (weaponless) hand. The term Karate-Do then refers merely to the "study of the way of the empty hand", and includes many of the golden lessons as described by Master Funakoshi. He also alluded to the notion that Kara carried a deeper meaning than just "Empty hand," in that the word "empty" also encompassed an empty, or pure, state of mind that desired no ill will towards others.

Kazumi Tabata

We have carried out considerable further study of original writings and scripts and discerned a much deeper significance hidden within the Japanese characters for "Empty hand." The key to this revelation was our knowledge that the character for "Kara" can also be pronounced as "Ku." "Ku" does not merely refer to "Empty" as in “empty space”, but also can indicate the soul, which is comprised of non-physical energy – energy which can be seen or sensed only by our inner eye. The following calligraphy presents "Kara Te Do," using those characters, set forth by Funakoshi, that refer to "Empty Hand Way" (i.e., “the way of the empty hand”). In the diagrams that follow, we will examine in detail the full composite meaning and derivation of each of these characters. As we do so, the reader will witness that a much deeper meaning for Karate-Do, that refers to the seamless connection of Body and Soul, that is inherent within the characters themselves. The Western reader should keep in mind that characters are actually pictorial in origin, and although simplified, present portions of their meaning in a diagrammatic manner unlike alphabetized writing.

Let us begin with "Kara," or "Ku." This character is composed of three distinct portions as indicated in the following diagram. The top-most portion, a curved stroke, depicts the Universe as a sort of "ceiling" or "heaven." The middle portion, consisting of similar left and right vertically-tilted strokes, is meant to depict "balance." The lower portion is meant to depict "create." Taken together, the strokes of this character refer to the Soul.

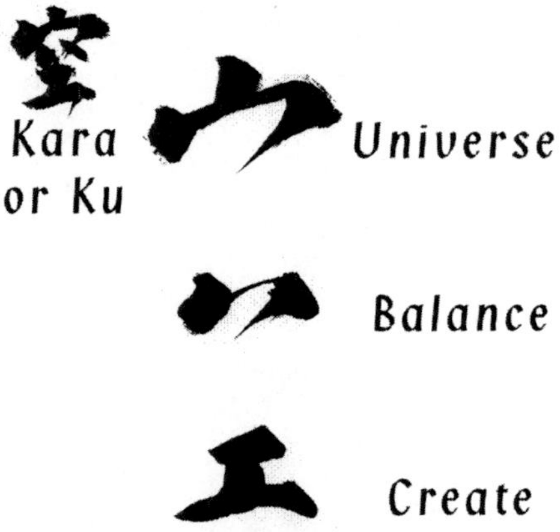

Let us now continue with an analysis of "Te." The three horizontal strokes of this character refer respectively to the Universe or the Heavens (top-most stroke), the Human body/soul (middle stroke), and, finally, the Earth (bottom stroke). The vertical stroke of this character passes through the center of all of these, connecting them, and suggests imparting a balance to the three of these elements.

Taken together, the strokes of this character refer to the Body. However, this is a body not in isolation, but one that lies between the Heavens and the Earth, and is, even if the individual is unaware, intimately connected to both.

It is apparent from these analyses that "Kara-Te" encompasses a unification of the soul and the body. Let us now examine closely the character, "Do," for an understanding of the true essence of "KaraTe-Do." The following diagram indicates how the character "Do" is comprised of three parts. The top-most strokes depict a balanced Universe, or Heaven. The central portion depicts an all-seeing eye – all-seeing in that the three areas enclosed within represent Heaven, the Soul and Earth, respectively. The lower-most portion depicts "direction." Taken together, this character, known simply as "the Way" encompasses an understanding of "the Way" in reference to all things in the Universe; an enlightened understanding of an art in relation to all arts, not in isolation.

Accordingly, "KaraTe-Do" in its deepest meaning refers to "A Life-Long Devotion To Understanding The Balance Of Body And Soul".

What are we to make of this deeper meaning of KaraTe-Do? We consider, simply, that it represents an opening of our eyes to what was there all along. While the Truth does not change, what is inherent to man is that his ability to grasp more of the Truth changes as he progresses throughout life, both as an individual as well as Mankind as a whole. All arts and sciences develop as Man progresses, and Karate is no exception. We have witnessed how certain basic Karate movements have been refined through continued analysis. Traditional Kata are passed on, but often develop and evolve over time. The art of ShotoKan was synthesized by Funakoshi from the sometimes diverse precepts and techniques of his two Master Instructors. The method in which we instruct our students must sometimes adapt to contemporary situations while still remaining rooted in tradition.

We will forever wonder whether the full realization of this deeper meaning of KaraTe-Do was well known to Master Funakoshi. It is possible, even likely, that he purposely revealed only a small part of its full significance when he described how "Kara" referred to "Empty," knowing that his students were not at the time ready to appreciate the deeper, secret meaning to Karate that we have described herein. It is also possible that the full extent of this deeper level of understanding was not entirely clear at the time even to him, and was perhaps subconsciously driven by his spirit in the hopes that it would later be revealed as it has been herein. Should this be the case, it is nevertheless due entirely to his foresight and devotion to the art that this deeper meaning of Karate has finally come to light.

CHAPTER 7

Mastery of Karate, Mastery of Oneself

To attain a level of competency in basic Karate techniques requires many years of practice. Mastery of karate, however, lies far beyond simple practice of techniques. To attain mastery, the student must progress through a lengthy process, which can be divided into three overall levels.

Initially, the student must devote his/herself to the process of *learning*. This involves little more than copying and memorizing techniques as presented by the teacher. It should be noted that inherent in this level is trust in the teacher. Once techniques have been committed to memory, years and years of repetition is required; this training period can be characterized as the second level. Only after the student has devoted sufficient attention to repetition can he/she progress to the third level, where personalization of techniques begins. Here the student molds these techniques to their own body and mind. This level does not involve discarding of teachings, but rather personal refinement, adaptation and contriving.

Many students progress well through the first and into the second levels of training, but do not manage to progress further. Such individuals who do not progress to the third level are essentially tacticians. They unfortunately remain focused only on victory and/or defeat. Such focus "traps" the mind, and actually slows down, rather than facilitates, the execution of techniques. Techniques cannot be truly effective if one's mind is filled such doubt and confusion. Only utter confidence in oneself, and a free and clear mind, will allow maximum power and effectiveness of techniques.

Rather than focusing on techniques or worrying about the outcome of an encounter, one should strive to maintain calm. One should not underestimate an opponent, but nevertheless assume a positive outcome. It can help to visualize one's opponent as a mere handful of dust. One should attempt to perceive the opponent's true intention in order to judge his/her own response level. All the while, one must minimize one's own fear and elevate courage. This can perhaps best be described as bringing one's insides (courage) out, and pushing one's outside (fear, uncertainty) in. One's opponent may lose fighting intent when confronted with such a formidable image.

One should never start a fight, nor engage in a meaningless encounter. However, to achieve victory should a life-or-death situation arise, one has to be willing to risk one's life in the process. Only then will he/she commit enough to the execution of techniques to be victorious.

Inherent in the students progress towards mastery, he/she must follow teachings as closely and accurately as possible, maintain a tranquil mind, and develop the presence of mind that enables free execution of techniques. This presence of mind is a state where one's mind is empty of distractions and is focused on a single goal. A true master approaches all aspects of life with such an attitude.

It is easy to state that one should have a free and clear mind. However, attainment of this state is difficult to achieve. Let us consider some of the aspects one must develop to attain such a presence of mind.

Fear is a natural instinct, but it limits, and can even paralyze, one's abilities. If one can manage to discard fear of death, one can fight with amazing ferocity. Beyond considerations of combat, one can never fully taste the delight offered by life when they are trapped by fear. One must realize that, happiness and misfortune, and even life and death, co-exist. One should strive not to be attached to either. True peace of mind exists only within one's mind itself. While it is not necessary to attempt to live like a saint, one should maximize devotion of one's energies to good causes. One can approach this goal by treating each day as if it were one's last. There is no better time to begin than now, and this time may never come again.

Following are some simple steps towards freeing one's mind that can be used throughout the day:

1. *Relax your shoulders, and your mind will settle.*
2. *When you are hasty, close your eyes and relax your thoughts.*
3. *When you are unable to make a decision, look up at the sky.*
4. *When you are in sorrow, stretch your back.*

One who trains for a period of time in karate, even at the technical level only, develops considerable power beyond that of average individuals. How one handles and develops this newfound power is important. Legend tells of three types of swords, which can represent one's karate. First, there is the Sword of God, which controls vandals, maintains the four seasons, and sustains the life of the universe. It can tear clouds in the sky and cut the ground in half. When this sword is raised, all leaders on earth halt and listen. Secondly, there is the Sword of Kings, which is forged of intelligence, bravery, loyalty and courage. This sword never loses a battle. This sword calms the minds of people and brings friendship and peace to all nations. Finally, there is the Sword of the Unenlightened, which always looks for meaningless trouble. It cuts through necks and cuts out hearts without control. Once it loses a battle, it is totally lost, and hurts, rather than helps, nations. The Karate practitioner must consider which Sword he/she would like to develop by studying Karate.

One must make a serious effort to understand others, and to see issues from their point of view, if one wishes to succeed at very difficult tasks. One should work one's entire life with an empty and open mind, free from fear, anger and meaningless conflict. One should always put into practice the spirit of the bow, which promotes respect for all people. Such an approach modifies for the better one's entire life. Improvement in one's karate beyond that of a mere tactician is but a small aspect of the result.

Mastery of Karate involves much more than techniques. The term Karate-Do is often used to describe life-long practice and incorporation of principles of Karate to one's entire life. There is yet a deeper level of understanding of Karate-Do. As described in the prior section, the word Karate itself is a composite, derived from Kara (empty) and te (hand). The simplest level of interpretation is in reference to an empty (weaponless) hand. The term Karate-Do then refers merely to the "study of the way of the empty hand", and includes many of the golden lessons as described by Master Funakoshi. While certainly admirable, there are yet deeper to Karate-Do. The Japanese character for Kara, also referred to as Ku, does not merely refer to "empty space", but also can indicate the soul, which is comprised of non-physical energy, energy which can be seen or sensed only by our inner eye. The character "te", in a larger sense, refers to physical aspects, or body. Kara-te can therefore refer to a unification or harmony between body and soul. Finally, Do can in a large sense refer to understanding or enlightenment. Accordingly, Karate-Do in its deepest meaning refers to an life-long devotion to understanding the balance of body and soul.

We began these discussions with consideration of three levels of Karate practice. However, it may be evident that such levels apply to one's entire life. We all have dreams, ambitions, and feelings.

Attaining a realistic grasp of one's own dreams, and developing realistic goals and approaches, is essential to achieving results. One can and should familiarize oneself with the sayings and writings of teachers and leaders of all walks of life, including religion, politics, philosophy, art, etc. This is analogous to the first level of Karate practice. One a degree of understanding has been achieved, one should study the finer aspects of their teachings and try to incorporate them into one's life. This is analogous to the years of practice of Karate techniques. However, just as one cannot progress beyond the level of a tactician in Karate without personalization of techniques, one should not forever merely "copy" or "parrot" the methods and teachings of others. One can achieve a profound level of peace and enlightenment by realistically applying one's own self to acquired teachings. As in mastery of Karate, this does not involve discarding aspects of a leader's teachings, nor does it advocate a "pick-and-choose" approach. Rather, one must realistically consider one's place in the world, one's own abilities, understand one's own feelings, and incorporate these aspects of oneself into what he/she has learned. Failure to move into this last level leaves one essentially being controlled by others, and never actually knowing oneself. Merely dreaming of success, or failing to realistically adjust one's approach to one's physical situation in life will bring neither success nor peace. This would be like dreaming of improving in Karate but never actually practicing techniques. As in Karate practice, one should set realistic goals and devote his/her self to them.

Each person, be they rich, poor, strong, weak, be they from whatever walk of life, must keep in mind that they actually represent the center of their own universe – that is to say, that anyone is just as important as all others around them. In fact, were he or she not born, then none of the people or experiences that he/she encounters would exist. All that he/she learns from anyone, no matter how lofty or learned that teacher or leader may be, cannot surpass what he/she has to offer. Every person's soul is like a flower, which is meant to blossom throughout life. If the student is able to understand him/herself fully, and can incorporate his/her own self into what he/she has learned, this student can eventually become a teacher.

Chapter 8
The Legend of Ju Gyu:

About 900 years ago in Sheung Tak Fu, China, the Buddhist sage Kok Yim Ci Yuen was saddened that the world had fallen away from spiritual enlightenment, and had become mired in the physical world. He presented the following beautiful and insightful story as a guide, to allow one to measure progress along their way towards spiritual enlightenment.

Stage 1: A confused boy, in his search for the cow (which represents to him enlightenment), heads into the forest. He of course does not find the cow there, and is consumed with worry. He is lost and needs guidance.

This corresponds to Shodan, where the new black belt has some technique and knows that he must seek guidance and cannot advance effectively on his own.

Stage 2: The boy searches diligently and finds a footprint! He feels like he has found a textbook that he can study and gain knowledge.

This corresponds to Nidan, 2nd degree black belt, where the individual tries to attain further knowledge from any source, not necessarily the best source.

<u>Stage 3:</u> The boy finds the cow, but can only see half of the cow at any time.

This corresponds to Sandan, where the individual begins to understand nature, but can really comprehend only a portion of nature and life.

<u>Stage 4:</u> The boy catches the cow, and can see all of the cow. But he still has trouble, as he cannot control the cow. The cow refuses to obey him.

This corresponds to Yodan, where the individual feels at times like he understands nature and himself, yet this understanding seems to slip through his fingers like smoke. He remains confused at times.

Stage 5: Here the boy begins to learn to control the cow. He cares for and nourishes it.

This corresponds to Godan, master level, where the individual begins to comprehend truth. He still has much to learn, however.

Stage 6: Here the boy controls the cow completely - he can ride on the cow, and the cow will do his bidding. He relaxes completely and plays the flute while riding, as he no longer even has to cling to the cow.

This stage corresponds to Rokyudan, where one day feels like an entire lifetime. The individual can relax and live a natural life without worry, without thinking.

Stage 7: Something new occurs here. The boy is alone - he doesn't seek the cow. Up until now he considered the cow as his quest, as his source of enlightenment. Now he realizes that enlightenment is within himself.

This stage corresponds to Sichidan, where the individual begins to find enlightenment within himself, where his body and mind meld into one, where true happiness comes to him naturally.

Stage 8: The boy has forgotten completely about the cow. In fact, he has in a way forgotten about everyone and everything. At this stage everything is one, all is equal and nature is balanced to him.

This stage corresponds to Hachidan, where the individual's mind is never disturbed regardless of the circumstances.

Stage 9: Up until now (Stages 1-8), we have witnessed the boy working hard, training, learning and preparing for practice of what is to come. Now, with this stage, we enter a new spiritual level, where the time for training has passed. Here the boy is a newborn, with no concerns, worries or distractions. He lives in a spiritual stage, and life feels perfect.

This stage corresponds to Kudan, where enlightenment and unenlightenment merely blend into a circle - he no longer even considers the need for enlightenment.

Stage 10: This final stage is where the boy uses his own enlightenment for the good of others. He lives much like a saint, where he moves through a world that is purely spiritual, and he exists only to help others. In this image, the boy, having attained enlightenment, is represented as the old Sage on the left, who is helping yet another boy begin his own journey.

This stage corresponds to Judan, 10th degree black belt.

Kazumi Tabata

CHAPTER 9
Knowledge of Mind

1. Good relationships Maintain your own health by keeping good relationships with others. To accomplish this: You have to maintain an open mind. You have to understand others' sadness. You should always try to help others.

2. Busyness Be careful of crowding your mind with unimportant things. Protect the time needed for meditation and contemplation.

3. Jealousy You must abstain from jealousy. You should not make people abide by your likes and dislikes. You should remember that there is destiny and the law of heaven. You can reduce jealousy by understanding the fact of density.

4. Anger Be careful with anger, since it can rob you of the ability to control yourself. If you lose control of yourself, you cannot help yourself or others, and you will become mentally ill.

5. Delusion Be careful about Delusion. When you have delusions, you should take a rest. Stray thoughts will be dissipate, and you will feel much better. You can improve your mental health by taking a rest.

6. Eating and Drinking You would improve your health if you cut down too much on your eating and drinking. People succumbed easily to temptation of food. You must make sincere efforts to defeat your greed.

7. Social Intercourse It is important to keep social intercourse within bounds. You should abstain from too much social intercourse in everyday life. Social intercourse is like labor, and too much can deprive you of vigor.

8. Gossip Do not believe gossip. Gossip seduces people and warps their judgment.

9. Etiquette KarateDo begins and ends with etiquette. Etiquette is the most important as the core of encounter between people. Etiquette is to express mind with attitude as form. There are many ways to show etiquette. Each attitude should have affection, respect for yourself and others. Luxury, arrogance and laziness arise when people forget etiquette. A great man said, "**KOUBE WO TARASU INAHO KANA.**" This means "An ear of rice hangs down because of weight of its golden seed." You should practice asceticism modestly by being generous and virtue, and by improving own technique and mind. Etiquette is one of the most important in relationship between people, between teacher and student, between sibling, between parents and children.

10. Five Precepts to help you achieve your goals Human beings are weak. People tend to choose easy road. Do not forget that you cannot achieve your goal without hardship. *In order to reach your goal:*

1. **Do not run away**
2. **Do not give up**
3. **Do not cheat**
4. **Do not be lazy**
5. **Do not make things complicated**

ACKNOWLEDGMENTS

I would like to extend my gratitude to the following individuals, presented in alphabetical order, who assisted to varying degrees in the preparation of this book:

Jim Ambrose	Miri Arai	Melissa Briscoe
Gregory Cummings	Jaimee Itagaki	Ted Fowler
Kyogi Kasao	Martin Katcoff	Arthur Kerr
Nakajima Kimiteru	Kanae Koh	Katusniko Maruoka
Nagao Matsuyama	Tom Shea	Danny Silvero

Special gratitude is expressed to my instructor, Professor Isao Obata, for his teachings and encouragement and to the past and present Instructors of the North American Karate Federation & the New England Collegiate Karate Conference:

John Almeida	James Ambrose	Jeremy Bailey
Princeton Bailey	Jordan Berry	Charles Butterfield
Cosmo Capobianco	Stuart Chassen	Bill Charles
David D'Amore	Gayle Spadafora Fleming	Ted Fowler
Dan Cheron	Bob Gomes	Bob Griffin
Robert Harb	Oscar Lightbourne	Malte Loos
Nagao Matsuyama	Cosmo Nardella	Ken Nishitane
George Noone	Bob Perrin	Tom Shea
Richard Sheehan	John Shirley	Vernon Simons
Andrea Tondo	Roger Trimm	Paget Wharton
Dwayne Williams		

About the Author Kazumi Tabata, a GrandMaster in the Shotokan and Shorinji styles of Karate, was sent to this country in the 60's by his teacher, Professor and Master Isao Obata, to promote Karate in the United States. Shortly after his arrival in this country, he established, and still serves as the Chief Instructor of, the North American Karate Foundation (NAKF) and the New England Collegiate Karate Conference (NECKC), both of which are based in Boston, Massachusetts. The NECKC is comprised of clubs throughout New England and New York. The NAKF is made up of private schools taught by Master Tabata's senior students. Master Tabata is the Chief Instructor and Coach of the Bermuda National Team, which regularly competes in the World Union Karate-Do Organization championships. Over the years, Master Tabata has a wide impact on the martial arts, ranging from training the local Tactical Police Force to hosting the first Boston-Asian Festival.

His philosophical insights are available in two books, "Secret Tactics" and "Mind Power," both available directly from Tuttle Publishing (www.tuttlepublishing.com) or from Amazon.com.

Printed in the USA/Agawam, MA